M

"With the world's attention focused on ongoing conflicts in Israel, journalists, authors, and scholars have examined the long-standing hostility between Jews and Muslims there. One group that is often omitted from the story, however, is the region's Christians. . . . In *Who Are the Christians in the Middle East?* Betty Jane and J. Martin Bailey explore the history of the region's various Christian groups, which include many different Orthodox, Catholic, and Protestant traditions. This is a very practical reference book. . . . The material is accessibly written and well researched."

— *Publishers Weekly*

"This remarkable book is a valuable reference on the historic churches of the Middle East. It also serves as a guidebook for travelers eager to understand and worship with fellow Christians in the region. For students of religion, this book enriches our understanding of the faith. For believers, it is a journey to the land where it all began. We are indebted to the Baileys for sharing their years of experience in the land we call 'holy' and for doing so in such a readable, informative fashion."

— **JAMES M. WALL**
senior contributing editor,
The Christian Century

"For many American Christians who see the Holy Land as a tourist destination, an archaeological site, or the place of bloody confrontation between Muslims and Jews, Betty and Martin Bailey's depiction of the churches in the Middle East will be startling. This description of the region's diverse Christian communities is both a helpful primer and a rich and affectionate portrait enabling readers to see beyond the media's images of intolerance, terror, and despair and to glimpse the human face of Christians persistently bearing witness to the gospel of hope, justice, and peace."

— **JOHN H. THOMAS**
former general minister and president,
Office of General Ministries,
United Church of Christ

Who Are the Christians in the Middle East?

• •

SECOND EDITION

Betty Jane Bailey & J. Martin Bailey

WILLIAM B. EERDMANS PUBLISHING COMPANY

GRAND RAPIDS, MICHIGAN / CAMBRIDGE, U.K.

First edition published 2003
Second edition published 2010

Wm. B. Eerdmans Publishing Co.
2140 Oak Industrial Drive N.E., Grand Rapids, Michigan 49505 /
P.O. Box 163, Cambridge CB3 9PU U.K.

Printed in the United States of America

15 14 13 12 11 10   7 6 5 4 3 2 1

Library of Congress Cataloging-in-Publication Data

Bailey, Betty Jane.
Who are the Christians in the Middle East? /
Betty Jane Bailey and J. Martin Bailey. — 2nd ed.
p.   cm.
Includes bibliographical references and index.
ISBN 978-0-8028-6595-3 (pbk.: alk. paper)
1. Christians — Middle East — History.
2. Church and state — Middle East — History.
3. Middle East — Church history.
I. Bailey, J. Martin, 1929-. II. Title.

BR1070.B25 2010

275.6 — dc22

2010008905

www.eerdmans.com

For Omar and Steve,
who married our daughters
and joined our extended family:

Omar taught us what growing up
in the Middle East means.

Steve knows everything about computers —
and has rescued us more than once.

Contents

III. Church and State in the Middle East

Preface to the Second Edition

It is now nearly a dozen years since the first edition of this book was prepared. A great deal has happened in the world in that period and the events have not been kind to the Middle East.

During those years we lived just a few miles away when the Twin Towers were destroyed and the world shuddered in the aftermath of Nine Eleven. We watched with horror as our country responded not only to those who planned the terrible attack but in Iraq as well. On our frequent visits to places like the Holy Land, to Jordan and to Lebanon, we learned how dramatically members of our family and close friends were affected.

Throughout the Middle East, the Christian churches reached out to hundreds of thousands of refugees who fled first from the horror of American bombs dropped in Iraq and then from the turmoil and anarchy that those bombs unleashed. In addition, the U.S. preoccupation with Iraq meant that efforts to achieve a just peace in Israel and Palestine were sidetracked and wars erupted between militarists in Israel and extremists in Lebanon and Gaza. The Christian churches in the Middle East, along with the United Nations and other peacemakers, have tried to pick up the pieces and minister to innocent victims. The churches of the region have carried on this ministry even when their own resources have been severely limited by turmoil and recession.

Dramatic changes throughout this region, along with increased interest on the part of Americans, some of whom have been sent there in uniform, have prompted us to update this book. The most obvious changes, we discovered, were in the names of leaders and in such details as addresses and telephone numbers. We have worked very hard to gather current information but in some cases we received confusing or even conflicting information.

We have also been struck by massive population shifts as emigration from the region has continued, most dramatically in the case of refugees from Iraq and parts of Sudan. We are deeply indebted for information supplied by several sources, most notably by Professor Bernard Sabella of Bethlehem University who is also a staff member of the Middle East Council of Churches. His research has gained wide recognition not only in Palestine but in Scandinavia and the United States as well. The Rev. Habib Badr, pastor of the National Evangelical Church in Beirut, shared his ecumenical vision with us.

There have been numerous changes in Part III, which deals with Church and State in the Middle East. The entire region is quite fluid and we have been grateful for substantive conversations and detailed correspondence from many sources. We need especially to acknowledge the assistance of three leaders of the Middle East Council of Churches, the General Secretary, Guirguis Ibrahim Saleh, an Egyptian, and two of his associates, the Rev. Nuhad Tomeh, whose assignments include Iraq, and Mr. Samer Laham of Damascus.

The enormous humanitarian needs caused by wars and the displacement of people have cut deeply into the resources of the churches of the Middle East and of their partners and friends in the United States and elsewhere. Because of this and other reasons the Middle East Council of Churches and several other organizations are being forced to alter their programs and structures. As this revised edition is being prepared, several changes are being contemplated that we have not been able fully to report. It is accurate to say, however, that the leaders and members of the Christian communities of the Middle East yearn not only for stability and peace but for the continued interest and prayers of friends and fellow believers around the globe.

BETTY JANE BAILEY AND J. MARTIN BAILEY
West Orange, New Jersey, U.S.A.
June 2010

Our Love Affair with the Middle East: An Introduction

In 1969, Everett Parker, the director of the United Church of Christ Office of Communication, concluded that the Middle East would soon be the most newsworthy place in the world. He organized a trip for journalists of Catholic and Protestant journals and magazines to several countries in the region, to meet church and government officials, media experts, and the leaders of various special interest groups. We went on that trip; it opened our eyes to the churches and politics of Egypt, Lebanon, Jordan, Israel/Palestine, and Turkey. (At the time, the Red Crescent society — the Muslim equivalent of the Red Cross — considered it unsafe for us to visit Syria.) On that journey, the walled Old City of Jerusalem worked its way into our hearts, and we vowed to go back.

It wasn't until 1982 that the opportunity arose again. In the midst of Israel's invasion of Lebanon, we traveled to the Middle East. Unlike the first time, our relatives were dubious and worried about our safety, and we had to assure them we would not go to Beirut by boat from Cyprus — the only practical way at the time. We again visited Egypt, Turkey, Jordan, and Israel-Palestine, and that time we also went to Syria. The trip resulted in continuing friendships as well as in stories and pictures of people who were involved in interfaith relations. Our work was published as a special issue of *A.D.* magazine called "The Bible Lands Today." The Old City of Jerusalem again claimed our hearts.

Then in 1990, Betty enjoyed a sabbatical leave at Tantur Ecumenical Institute in Jerusalem. Mart was able to join her for ten days. By then she considered the Old City a second home; she knew the narrow streets and she forged friendships with clergy in the churches, shop-

keepers in the souk, and even a few food vendors in places like the fala-
fel shop near the Western Wall. After that experience, it was easy for us
to decide that we would spend our retirement working with the Christian communities in the area and on Middle East issues of peace and
justice. To prepare for that, Betty spent an academic year at Columbia
University studying about the region.

In October 1994 we moved to Jerusalem, where we worked as volun-
teers — Betty at Tantur and Mart with the Middle East Council of
Churches. In 1996 we moved to Bethlehem in the occupied West Bank;
both of us served at the MECC's Jerusalem Liaison Office, commuting
daily through an Israeli military checkpoint. While we were there, we
began researching this book. We also learned a bit of Arabic and what it
means to be part of a Christian minority. As we drove to church in Jerusalem each Sunday we would see Jewish families hanging out their
"Monday wash." We became conscious of the religion of storekeepers
as we discovered which days they were closed for their sabbaths. And we
learned to avoid the crushing crowds at 1 P.M. on Fridays in the Old
City when the prayers at the Al Aksa mosque ended.

After returning to the United States in 1998 we were ready to devote
the rest of our lives to issues relating to the Middle East. We recalled
how poorly prepared we had been in 1969 and even in 1982 to understand the three faiths and the two peoples in the Holy Land. So we began to prepare resources to help others get behind the headlines from
the region. We agreed that if we could start seminary again we would
devote more time to church history and patristics. Alas! Those are areas
many people begin to appreciate only as they mature and accumulate
experience.

That brings us to the intent of this book. This small volume is designed to introduce non-seminarians and non-academics (and perhaps
some seminarians and academics as well) to the Christians and the
churches of the Middle East, and to the circumstances in which they
live out their vocations. We know that while some will read this book in
its entirety, others will use it as a reference book to "look up" a particular church, country, or holy site; for this reason it seemed best to make
each section relatively self-contained, even if this resulted in the occasional repetition of information in the book as a whole. We have attempted to simplify centuries of church history and to unravel the tan-
gles and intrigues of church relations, and we have sought to do this in

language familiar to Western Christians. We have struggled with the fact that official names of denominations are translated into English in different ways by different people. We have come to terms with the fact that any references to the Arabic have been transliterated, with four or five possible spellings. We have checked and double-checked addresses, phone and fax numbers, e-mail addresses, and website *urls,* hoping that interested persons may follow up with direct contacts. We have tried to be fair as we describe churches with only a few centuries of history and those with vivid memories going back two millennia. We hope what we have written will encourage people to read other books, to visit the region, to experience other religious traditions, and to appreciate the richness of the universal church. We also hope that readers will choose to befriend the indigenous Christians of the East.

We frequently meet people who are surprised to learn that Christians still live in the Middle East. Some believe that Islam has completely replaced Christianity. Others assume that today's Christians are the product of relatively recent missionary activity. Most people are unaware, until they think about it, that the church was born in the East; few would guess that there are still Christian communities that trace their roots to the disciples of Jesus and the day of Pentecost. Almost none realize that in the minds of many Middle Easterners all the centuries co-exist, directly affecting their emotions and their decisions. We have learned that tradition is not old fashioned; it is a way of getting closer to Jesus and the biblical story. Traditions do not preserve the old ways; they make it possible to draw from the deep wells of our faith.

Our experiences and our writing assignments have rewarded us with a very rich ecumenical experience. We have worshiped using many different liturgies and in several different languages. We have come to value the universal church that exists not only in different places but also in different times. The presence of the saints in icons has enhanced our sense of *the* church. Christians from every time and place are present with us in the liturgies, the symbols, and the music of both ancient and contemporary churches.

We are grateful to the Middle East Council of Churches for making it possible for us to travel throughout the region, attending conferences and meeting with many leaders of churches, including patriarchs and the Coptic pope. With few exceptions, the basis of our writing comes from personal experience and interviews, together with books and articles given to us by men and women in offices, churches, monasteries, and assembly rooms. The MECC enabled us to meet all but one of the persons we have described in the vignettes in Part II of the book and to visit most of the sites included in Part III.

As we assembled materials for this book, two persons who became good friends agreed to share their own perceptions. David Kerr has described his own affection for the ancient churches, an appreciation that has developed over decades. Perhaps no individual is better equipped than Riad Jarjour to evaluate the recent experiences of Middle East Christians and to project the future of the church in the region. We are especially grateful to Riad and his wife, Roseangela, to the general secretaries of the MECC, and to the Fellowship of Middle East Evangelical Churches for their support of this project and for their own commitment to the churches we learned to love. They helped us in innumerable ways. Lew and Nancy Scudder, who live in Cyprus, offered copious information and wondrous hospitality — along with a calming approach to the Middle Eastern style. Thanks also go to Afaf Deeb Kandis of the MECC's Beirut office for bits and pieces of information that she supplied as she edited the Arabic version of *Christianity through its History in the Middle East.* (That massive book, now available in English, was written by Middle Eastern Christians from their own perspectives. It will be a valuable resource for those — many, we hope — who become more interested in the subject as they read this book.)

While we are enormously grateful to them and dozens of others who generously gave us their time and willingly shared the wisdom of their own experiences, we of course assume full responsibility for what we have written. This book ultimately represents the views of two American Protestants, though we eagerly acknowledge that our experiences in the Middle East have enriched our lives and broadened our lifelong ecumenical commitments.

BETTY JANE BAILEY AND J. MARTIN BAILEY
West Orange, New Jersey, U.S.A.
July 2002

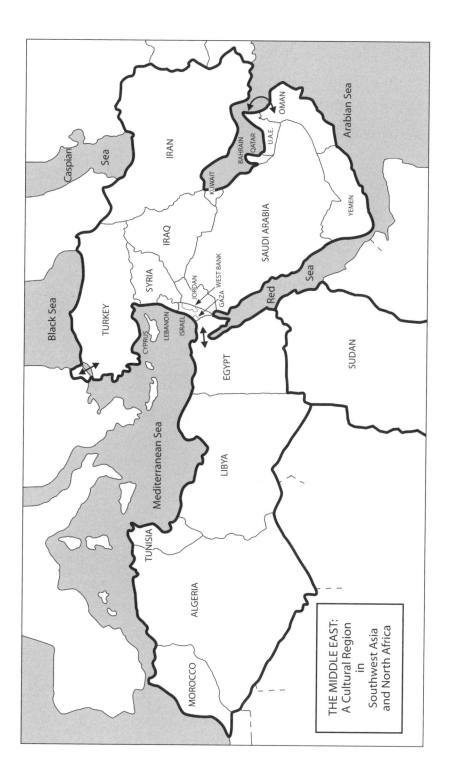

THE MIDDLE EAST:
A Cultural Region
in
Southwest Asia
and North Africa

PART I

THE CHURCHES OF THE MIDDLE EAST

A Western Christian Appreciation
of Eastern Christianity

DAVID A. KERR

In planning this book, we were aware that many Western Christians have negative or distorted impressions of Eastern Christianity, often due to ignorance of the place of Eastern Christianity in the history of our faith. We asked Professor David Kerr, a frequent visitor to the Middle East, to help Western readers appreciate the role of and gifts from this important branch of the worldwide church.

Calling Us Back to the New Testament

To walk through the ancient walled city in East Jerusalem is an experience I always treasure. The jostling crowds of Palestinian merchants, Christian clerics from churches strange and familiar, Muslim imams and Jewish rabbis, international tourists, intimidating and no doubt intimidated soldiers — all mingle in a bedlam that defies pious stereotypes of a holy place but brings to life the human accents of Jerusalem in the New Testament.

Then there is the stunning array of architecture: Syriac churches

---

David A. Kerr was Professor of Christianity in the Non-Western World at the University of Edinburgh, Scotland, when this essay was written. He had also served as director of the Macdonald Center for the Study of Islam and Christian-Muslim Relations at Hartford Seminary, Hartford, Connecticut. At the time of his death in 2008 he was teaching missiology and ecumenics at Lund University in Sweden.

that witness the earliest development of Christianity in the region; Armenian churches in the style of the earliest Christian pilgrims to Jerusalem; churches in the Orthodox style of the Byzantine Greeks who built so much of the original Christian architecture of the holy city; the Coptic and Ethiopian churches representing the ancient pilgrimage tradition of African Christianity; the Latin architectural styles of medieval Catholic crusaders and of the Franciscan mission in the *Terra Sancta;* and the Western-style churches of the Anglican, Lutheran, and Reformed traditions, relative late-comers to Jerusalem.

To encounter such immense diversity within the crowded space of a small town can be a confusing experience. But to survey the Old City from one of the surrounding hills — my favorite is the quiet vantage point of the Dominus Flevit chapel on the Mount of Olives[1] — is a unique way of visualizing world Christianity in this uniquely global village.

Standing there always confronts me with an intensely personal question: how has my Western Christian identity been influenced by the Christianity I have encountered in the Eastern churches? To attempt to answer this question in a short essay — without being too personal — may suggest to the reader how the Middle Eastern churches, so little known in some other regions, have made an essential contribution to world Christianity.

The Heirs of Pentecost

The picture I have tried to paint of contemporary Jerusalem takes us back to the very beginnings of the church on the day of Pentecost as recorded in the Acts of the Apostles:

> And at this sound the crowd gathered and was bewildered, because each one heard them speaking in the native language of each. Amazed and astonished, they asked, "Are not all these who are speaking Galileans? And how is it that we hear, each of us, in

---

1. Luke 19:41-42: "As [Jesus] came near [Jerusalem] and saw the city, he wept over it, saying, 'If you, even you, had only recognized on this day the things that make for peace!'"

4

our own native language? Parthians, Medes, Elamites, and residents of Mesopotamia, Judea and Cappadocia, Pontus and Asia, Phrygia and Pamphylia, Egypt and the parts of Libya belonging to Cyrene, and visitors from Rome, both Jews and proselytes, Cretans and Arabs — in our own languages we hear them speaking about God's deeds of power." All were amazed and perplexed, saying to one another, "What does this mean?" (Acts 2:6-12)

Bewildered, amazed, astonished, perplexed — the experience of the first Christians may have been little different from ours. Gathered in Jerusalem from their many lands, these first Christians had a miraculous experience of unity in their common faith in Jesus Christ as God's Spirit poured out on all who were present (Acts 2:18).

The early church was multi-lingual and multi-ethnic, just as are the churches of the Middle East today. They remind us that Christianity from its very beginnings has included peoples of many languages and cultures. They remind us also that the Western experience of Christianity, be it Catholic or Protestant, is but a portion of the much greater whole. Those who gathered at Pentecost came in greatest number from places in Asia and Africa. The "visitors from Rome" were evidently few among the many.

The Middle East in its later history has never relinquished its early marks of Christian diversity. But the many different churches have found it more difficult to express the unity of faith that bound the earliest followers of Christ in a single spirit. Theological disagreements, the Muslim imposition of *dhimmi* status on Christians,[2] the entrance of the crusaders, and, in Israel, laws inherited in part from earlier rulers, both Muslim and Christian, perpetuate these differences.[3]

Apostles and Peoples

From Jerusalem the first Christians took the gospel to their own lands. In doing so they gave Christianity its enduring character as an evange-

2. For an explanation of *dhimmi* status, see the boxed text on p. 54.

3. For a country-by-country analysis of the circumstances in which Christians are currently living, see Part III.

lizing faith. The Bible attributes the work of evangelism to the apostles — the Greek word *apostolos* means "messenger." The original apostles mentioned in the New Testament were Jesus' original twelve disciples. To their number were added Matthias, Paul, and Barnabas.

In terms of the missionary growth of the church, Western Christians first think of the apostle Paul and his missionary journeys through the Mediterranean recorded in the New Testament. For many Eastern Christians the apostle Thomas is quite as important, for they regard him as the one who preached the gospel among the "Parthians, Medes, Elamites, and residents of Mesopotamia" (Acts 2:9) and onward to India. The apostle Mark is similarly honored by the Christians "of Egypt and the parts of Libya belonging to Cyrene" (Acts 2:10) as the missionary to Egypt and the founder of the Coptic Church. The apostle Thaddaeus (also known as Jude) may have been sent by Thomas to the desert kingdom of Edessa in northern Mesopotamia, where Middle Eastern Christians celebrate his healing of the Arab King Abgar and his conversion of Abgar's people. Together with Bartholomew, Thaddaeus also is claimed by the Armenians as one of the first apostles to Armenia.

Though these ancient legends may lack historical certitude, they remind us that Christianity is by nature a missionary faith. The missionary apostles were not, however, "foreign missionaries" in the Western sense of this term. They preached the gospel and planted the Kingdom of God among their *own* peoples. Christianity consequently became an inseparable part of the identity of the nations to which they belonged. King Abgar's conversion in the first century A.D. would make his tribal domain of Edessa the first Christian kingdom in history. With surer grounding in historical records, Armenians claim this distinction for their third-century king Tiridates III (c. 238-314), who was converted by Gregory the Illuminator, the Apostle of Armenia — the honor of apostle by this time being accorded to the leader of Christian mission in any nation. In a similar way the conversion of the Emperor Constantine confirmed the progressive Christianization of the Byzantine Empire from the fourth century A.D. on.

Churches and Nations

This pattern of conversion in which entire peoples adopted the religion of their national leader provides a historical precedent for the medieval Western Christian principle that "the prince's religion reigns in the prince's land" *(cuius regio, eius religio)*. In its Eastern origins, however, this was not a matter of political expedience as in medieval Europe. It points, rather, to the Eastern understanding of the church as "local" to the life of its people — indigenous, and identified with the nation. It is "the anchor of the nation's existence," as Aram I, the Catholicos of Cilicia in the Armenian Apostolic Church, puts it.[4]

The value of this principle proved itself again and again in the history of the Eastern churches. When peoples lost their political statehood, the churches continued as guardians of their nation's identity. This happened when much of the Middle East fell under the rule of the Byzantine Empire and later under the Islamic Caliphate. Through these vicissitudes the churches continued to embody the faith of their nations, when the latter lost their political reality. These national/religious identities still exist today in Western diaspora when local churches put on ethnic festivals and when they hold language schools to teach the children and youth to speak and understand the "mother" tongue.

Liturgy, Worship, and Witness

This continuing ethnic identity, when the nation no longer existed, shows that the strength of the churches did not depend on the political apparatus of states. Rather, as Eastern Christians themselves emphasize, the peoples' Christian identity rested upon the importance of "liturgy" in their lives, often sustained by martyrdom as the ultimate way of witness.

The English word "liturgy" (Greek *leitourgia*) comes from the Greek words for "people" *(laos)* and "service" *(ergon)*. Liturgy means the service that the people render to God and to their fellow people. Through

---

4. This quote, and others throughout the book that are not footnoted, is taken from conversations with the individuals quoted.

their liturgies the Eastern churches have sustained the faith of the apostles, indigenized in the cultures of their peoples through their vernacular languages, the regular commemoration of their martyrs, and the festivals of their communities.

Syriac Christians trace their liturgy to the apostle James, brother of Jesus, and use the ancient Syriac language. From the Syriac liturgy the fifth-century Armenian Saint Mesrob (d. 440) developed the Armenian liturgy, for which he devised the Armenian alphabet. The Coptic liturgies are derived from the apostle Mark, and from the later Greek theologians Basil the Great and Gregory Nazianzus. The liturgies we use today in our Western churches owe a debt to the forms and prayers that were preserved by the Eastern churches as well as by the Church of Rome.

Western Christians are often struck by the haunting beauty of these ancient Eastern liturgies. Eastern Christians remind us that this points to their spiritual intent. Emulating ancient Hebrew and other pre-Christian traditions of worship in the Middle East, these Christian liturgies are sung or chanted in order to beautify both the worship and

> Music is neither supplementary to, nor an enrichment of, worship. It is the expression of worship itself. It is not an accompaniment, a background, a preparation, a moodsetter, a filler, or any such thing, and it is certainly not a divertimento. Unless this is understood by those who sing in church, we will advance no further in our interpretation. Church music as an art can only be interpreted according to its own true liturgical function.
>
> Sergei Glagolev ("An Introduction to the Interpretation of Liturgical Music," *Orthodox Church Music*, no. 1 [1983], p. 25)

the worshiper. Eastern theology emphasizes that beauty is of the very nature of God. The liturgical experience of beauty enables the worshiper to experience God and to become God-like *(theosis)* — that is, to reflect the beautiful image of God within oneself. This in turn beautifies the life one leads.

The same purpose is served by the icons that are a feature of many, though not all, Eastern churches. It is said that the Arab King Abgar of Edessa invited Jesus to visit and heal him, but that Jesus, unable to come in person, sent an image of himself that restored the king to health. Whatever the truth of this story, its point is clear: an icon (the Greek word for "image") mediates the presence of the one whom it depicts. While the icon is never to be used as an object of worship, the

> For Orthodox Christians icons not only teach, they also make the persons who are pictured immediately present to the believer. Perhaps more accurately stated, they make the believer present to the Kingdom of God. [Orthodox Christians believe that] in all material things, human beings were not only intended to find satisfaction for their life needs but also to discover communion with God, the source of all joy. . . . [H]umans alone were given the gift of creativity to transfigure energy into spirit and thus to commune with God's spirit in whose image they were created. [In an icon] a piece of wood, with the use of other natural products, is transfigured into an image of God's grace. Matter is restored to its original purpose, that of bearing spirit and thus bringing communion and joy.
>
> For the believer, the icon has become a window to the Kingdom, a witness that things are not as they seem, that the world is not what it appears to be apart from faith.
>
> V. Bruce Rigdon ("Icons: Sermons in Color," *Concern Magazine* [April 1979]; published by United Presbyterian Women)

holy presence "imaged" in it may cleanse imperfections that sully the image of God within us.

If the liturgy of worship animates the collective identity of the people, the liturgy of service expresses the social outreach of their Christian faith. Education has always been a primary example of this second dimension of liturgy, and the leading educators through the centuries have been the monks. Devotion to the study of their liturgies and Scripture was complemented by commitment to extending literacy among their peoples. The churches took responsibility for schooling,

9

and the level of education among Eastern Christian communities was generally above the average of the rest of the population.

It is not surprising, therefore, that Christian scholars were found in the courts of Muslim rulers. In more recent times Christians have contributed enormously to the development of modern social and political thought in the Arab states that were created upon the collapse of the Ottoman Empire in the early twentieth century. The challenge with which Middle Eastern Christians wrestle today is to relate the gospel to "every nook and cranny" of the life of Arab nations.[5]

Indigenous Witness and Western Missions

The witness of the Middle Eastern churches has been both helped and hindered by Western Christians. The goal of education encouraged the Eastern churches to entertain closer relations with Western churches, especially as the latter extended their missionary outreach to the Middle East. Western educational support, however, often demanded its own price in the imposition of Western patterns of church order on the Eastern churches. The result was the proliferation of Catholic and Protestant churches for "converts" from the Eastern churches. From the perspective of the indigenous Eastern churches this was an unacceptable form of intra-Christian proselytism that continues to overshadow their attitudes toward Western concepts of Christian mission and church unity. The most important lesson we have to learn from this history is that the search for Christian unity must honor the fact that the many peoples of Christ each have their own Christian integrity. The spirit of Pentecost must be ours today. The Eastern churches remind us that Western Christianity cannot legitimately or effectively impose itself on others.

Christianity and Religious Pluralism

One of the many issues challenging Western Christians today is that of religious pluralism. How are we to live as neighbors to people of other

5. Ion Bria, ed., *Martyria/Mission: The Witness of the Orthodox Church* (Geneva: WCC Commission on World Mission and Evangelism, 1980), p. 228.

faiths who have either moved to or been born in Western societies? Jews have lived with Christians, often very uncomfortably, for centuries. But it is only recently in Western experience that Christians are learning to live with Muslims — now the second largest religious community in the West — and with many other so-called Eastern religions that are making a home in the West.

Middle Eastern Christians have a longer experience of Islam than do Christians in any other part of the world. It was in Arabia that Islam had its historical origins, and it was among the previously Christian regions of Syria, Iraq, and Egypt that Islam experienced its formative development. That Islam should have become the predominant religion throughout the region, shaping so much of its political, social, and cultural character, raises major questions for Christianity. In many ways the Christians best able to answer these questions are those that have the longest firsthand experience of the issues.

In the heart of the old city of Bethlehem, not far from the Church of the Nativity, an Arab Christian pastors a church in the midst of a largely Muslim population. "Islam," he writes, "has been the most significant component of the world of Arab Christianity for almost fourteen hundred years. Arab Christians and Muslims share the Arabic culture, history, and language; their fate is intertwined and inseparable. Likewise, Arab Christians are an inseparable part of the world of Islam. Dialogue with Muslims is a necessary and important aspect of Arab Christians' life and survival."[6]

This little church in Bethlehem serves the whole people, both Muslim and Christian. It gives hope to young people who find themselves caught between political polarities. It encourages Christians to continue to express their faith in a very difficult situation rather than emigrate to the West. It seeks to transcend borders and build bridges.

In this way Middle Eastern Christians embody the spirit of Christianity. They are loyal to their apostolic faith. They bring new life to the culture of their people. They radiate the gospel in seemingly hopeless political situations that inflict suffering on many. They nurture the Kingdom of God in community with Muslims and Jews. And they remind this writer of why he aspires to be Christian.

---

6. Mitri Raheb, *I Am a Palestinian Christian* (Minneapolis: Fortress, 1995), p. 9.

The Future of Christians in the Arab World

Are Christians in the Middle East dying out? Whenever the question about the future of Christians in the Arab world is raised, the answer always seems to be pessimistic. In a recent volume in the encyclopedic French series on the Christians of the East, Jean-Pierre Valognes asks,

> Will the final uprooting of the Christians from the East take the form of a tragedy? There are too many crude precedents for us to rule out that possibility. But in spite of everything, it is more likely that they will quietly disappear in the process of a draining away, a process at once both unobtrusive and merciless.[1]

Valognes is excessively pessimistic. I believe it is important to describe the reality that Christians in the Arab world face, including the challenges to their lives, the responses to these challenges, and the horizons of their future and destiny.

---

1. Jean-Pierre Valognes, *Vie et mort des chrétiens d'Orient: des origines à nos jours* (Paris: Fayard, 1994).

The Rev. Dr. Riad Jarjour, a former General Secretary of the Middle East Council of Churches, is currently General Secretary of the Arab Group for Muslim-Christian Dialogue and President of the Forum for Development, Culture and Dialogue. His office is in Beirut, Lebanon.

The Challenges Christians Face

1. The Middle East's Structure of Endemic Crisis

Since the mid-years of the First World War, when conspiracies were hatching for the division of the Middle East into a patchwork quilt of imperial domains, the region has been the playground of external manipulators. More recently, the success of religious fanatics throughout the region has neutralized the moderate center of Arab society and marginalized the communities that do not belong to the dominant ethno-religious groups. External forces manipulate societies that become less and less able to define their own identity and manage their own reality. The structure of endemic crisis is well established in the region.

In this environment, the potentials of the Middle East are being wasted. The region is greatly blessed with human and material resources. The people are creative and retain their gift of ingenuity. They are enterprising and productive. They create beauty and express humor. In ancient times, the Middle East was among the world's most wealthy regions in a material sense; in modern times, oil and other mineral resources have become major resources.

Middle Eastern communities, however, are being decimated, dispersed, depressed, and disempowered. The largest of the world's displaced and refugee communities are Middle Eastern. Material resources are being sold to the benefit of a select few, and the gap between rich and poor continues to grow. The church bears a heavy burden to work for justice, human rights, and respect for creation — a burden it cannot bear alone.

2. The Demographic Hemorrhage

Christians in the Middle East number between ten and twelve million. This is compared with one hundred and fifty million Muslims. This ratio is changing, and the decline in the number of Christians in the Middle East differs from country to country. Forty years ago Christians in Iraq made up 6 percent of the population; today they are less than 3 percent. Before the civil war in Lebanon began in 1975, Christians constituted half of the population; today they are about 33 percent. In 1948 Christians composed 50 percent of Jerusalem's residents; today they are not more than 3 percent and a significant number of these are expatriates.

Although the size of Christian families is smaller than that of Muslim families, the most obvious reason for decline is that Christians are emigrating more rapidly than Muslims, and in proportionally greater numbers, to countries outside the Arab world.

3. The Politicization of Religions

Political Islam threatens all Arab Christians. Its goal is to establish a Muslim religious state. In such a state Christians would be no better than resident aliens, guests, or, at best, second-class citizens. Although not all Muslim political organizations advocate the same goals, there still remains the notion of Islam as both religion and secular authority. Given circumstances of time, place, and power alignments, political Islam can lead to certain human rights violations, the most important of which is the right to equality.

Similarly, in Israel and occupied East Jerusalem, political Judaism has imposed an exclusivist claim to a land and a city that historically was not only spiritually important to the three Abrahamic faiths but also was the homeland for many Muslims and Christians. Since the formation of the Zionist state in 1948, Arab residents of Israel proper have been treated as second-class citizens and with great suspicion. Even the secular Jews in Israel feel mounting pressure as their state increasingly is dominated by religious parties. A variety of national policies have led both Christians and Muslims in areas controlled by Israel to feel unwelcome in the land of their birth.

Counteracting these movements requires a stronger and more insistent emphasis on concepts of "nation" and "patriotism" that are distinct from and not to be replaced by religious identity. Challenging political Islam and political Judaism also requires that the notion of "religion" be clarified and affirmed. Religious faith ought to be neither subject to nor exploited for political purposes. Religion's proper place is as a reasonable guide to God, the source and destiny of all that is; it is religion that gives life meaning.

4. The Western Intrusion of "Protectionism"

Western Christians might think that for many centuries and even today there is a special kinship tie between them and Eastern Christians and that Eastern Christians are not really Arabs. They do not understand that even in the Arabian Peninsula, Christianity was the environment within which Islam was born. Christianity preceded Islam. "It was in Antioch [now an Arab city] that the disciples were first called 'Christians'" (Acts 11:26).

Since the beginning of the last millennium, the West has intruded into the Middle East with its own particular interests. The pretext was always the same: "protection." The Western Crusades, which merged Western ecclesiastical and temporal interests, theoretically were launched to "protect" the holy places. In fact, they expressed more worldly political and economic interests and revealed a deep Western animosity against Eastern Christians. The Crusades planted in Muslim hearts the seeds of suspicion and doubt against their Christian compatriots, a persistent image that pictures Arab Christians as agents of a greedy West, a "fifth column" poised to stab Muslims in the back.

In modern times, European governments intervened under the slogan of "protecting minorities" in the Ottoman Empire. Then, as the empire declined and became the "sick man of Europe," the European powers swarmed over it, bickering among themselves about how to divide up the possessions of the sick man when he died.

Since 1948 the West has continued to manipulate religion as a factor in its policies. When the Western nations discovered that much of the oil they needed for industrial growth was buried in ground settled by Muslims, the relationship with the Middle East was decisively redefined. Economic, political, and strategic interests dictated that in this new framework there was no place for concern about Eastern Christians.

Christians were victims of a variant form of "protection" practiced for many centuries by Rome and, in later days, by Western Protestants. The latter's purpose was to evangelize or proselytize Eastern Christians. Assuming they could teach the Eastern Christians about Christ, Western churches reopened old wounds that still festered in the East. According to His Beatitude Patriarch Ignatios IV of Antioch, "They wanted to 'stimulate life' in the historic churches by incorporating them within Western ecclesiastical bodies."

Christian Reactions

Christians in the Arab world face these challenges in various ways and with varying degrees of intensity. Their reactions include the following:

1. Resignation

The reaction of resignation or despair is dominated by a feeling of despondency, which in turn can lead to a variety of actions. Arab Christians often fear that their circumstances may become worse than they are now. They may surrender, give up, capitulate. Even as citizens they accept anguish as normal and their inferior or marginalized status as unavoidable. Sometimes they do not even demand their rights, and some Christians respond by giving up their inherited religion.

The result of resignation for many people is to retreat emotionally to "the golden age" when people knew great happiness, unity, and prosperity. As present difficulties intensify, the heirs of that golden age escape into past glory, seeking to forget the bitterness of their present condition. They try to dissociate themselves from their present by living in a fantasy world.

A kind of physical divorce is also the result of resignation. To "go westward" *(al-ightirab)* is one alternative by which Arabs have chosen to avoid living together in tension and hammering out a common political life. In the past, Christians emigrated internally, but in the early years of the twentieth century most of those who emigrated headed westward. They had given up on the idea of trying to be a part of a coherent Arab society. These emigrations have become more or less final divorces.

2. Tribal Solidarity

Tribalism, as a reaction, is another form of resignation, but it represents the other side of the coin, leading to patterns of resistance that gradually become more intense. In all multi-religious and multi-ethnic societies, exclusivity is a natural option. When the peoples of the Middle East adopted Christianity, they were extremely tenacious in retaining their national cultures. The groups who opposed the doctrine declared in A.D. 451 by the ecumenical Council of Chalcedon were forced to distance themselves politically as well as theologically from the Byzantine Empire; they affirmed themselves as national churches.

With the Muslim conquest and the formulation of Muslim politics and theology, the greatest mass of Middle Eastern Christians became Muslim. Those who remained loyal to Christianity also preserved their ethnic heritages. In the matter of language they accommodated themselves to the Arab-Muslim reality, but they retained their original ancient languages in the context of their liturgies.

The *dhimmi* status given to Middle Eastern Christians under traditional Islamic government has always resulted in a "legal" reason for Middle Eastern Christians to preserve their exclusivity.[2] In a society that allowed for co-existence of Muslims and non-Muslims, the legal inequality of and restrictions on Christians and Jews led each of them to close ranks within their own communities. Even though today's modern sensibilities call for equality of social and legal status, the mentality and social practices of the past era still have repercussions.

Fundamentalism or sectarian extremism is another manifestation of tribal solidarity. Religious fundamentalism advocates a return to the Scriptures and to a "golden age" when religion is considered to have been pure. But religious fundamentalism quickly turns into sectarian extremism and becomes a political enterprise, as one religious sectarian extremism faces another religious sectarian extremism.

3. Living within the Tensions

Not all Christian reactions to the challenge of living in the Middle East are so extreme. Some Arab Christians avoid both the feelings of resignation and the patterns of resistance. Instead they struggle to live within the various tensions of their society.

The first tension is within Christianity itself. Christians belong to a specific local community of faith. They also belong to a denomination. Their local group represents a spiritual bond, a communion of the faithful, while the denomination is the social embodiment of the

2. For an explanation of *dhimmi* status, see the boxed text on p. 54.

church. The denomination is a sociocultural bloc, distinguishing itself from other blocs of the same kind, and defining its identity by its particular history. Christians ought not live out their loyalty to the local church at the expense of the denomination or vice versa. As they live within this tension Christians must find a middle road or accurately read the signs of the times to know when to focus on the local community of faith and when to focus on the wider community of faith. Similarly, all Christians also live with an ecumenical vocation. No part of the church can faithfully exist in any given place while it ignores or is at enmity with the other parts. Christians must seek ways of remaining loyal to their particular community of faith while expressing solidarity with all who follow Christ.

Some Christians feel torn between the spiritual and temporal dimensions as they live lives defined by their national belonging. When Arab Christians — even in Lebanon, for example — became minorities, they began to suffer as all minorities suffer in societies not built upon full secularism. Are they citizens who are equal (or should be equal) with all others? Or are they members of minorities whose status in society is defined by the sect to which they belong?

The third kind of tension that Christians in the Middle East experience is whether they belong to the Arab East, whose cultural features are defined by Islam, or whether they identify with a Western society that bears the historical stamp of Christianity. The culture of the Arab East has been shaped by its experience with and within the Muslim culture. Many Arab Christians feel that their fate is bound up with that of their Muslim compatriots. If they do not fully participate in this destiny, especially at critical fate-determining points, they must ask themselves about their relationships with the West.

Choices of Destiny

What good is it for Arab Christians to understand all of this if their awareness does not provide them scope to control their own destiny and to define what they must do with the options open to them? Christians in the Arab world face four choices that offer firm foundations for lives of dignity and freedom.

1. Liberation in Renewal

The most inclusive choice — one that can sum up all the choices — is the choice to seek "liberation in renewal." Liberation is the object; renewal is the means.

Today there are many reasons for anxiety, but the church in the Middle East has begun to take its destiny into its own hands. The Eastern churches are experiencing internal renewals, each in a manner relevant to its situation and with the goal of transcending present problems to move toward a brighter future. These renewals include renovations of buildings and institutions, youth movements, the revival of monastic life, dialogue with Islam, a measure of comfort in the Muslim world, and the deepening of indigenous roots.

The very real anxiety concerning the future of Christianity in the Middle East has gone beyond the fear that the Christian monuments in the region may someday become mere museums. The Christian community has come to see this issue in qualitative terms. Christian presence in the Middle East is now being expressed as an issue of Christian life and witness, and church leaders and people have taken upon themselves roles as ministers of mercy in the wider society. Already their work has produced fruits of tolerance and communal reconciliation.

Middle Eastern Christians also are seeing the need for more interactive and constructive relationships with Christians in other parts of the world. These relationships often provide encouragement for the local or regional churches in the Middle East, demonstrating that the Christians of this region are neither alone nor isolated but are part of a larger community of witness and compassion.

2. Muslim-Christian Dialogue

Within the Middle East, the future of the church is to live within an environment dominated by Muslims. Therefore, engaging in Muslim-Christian dialogue is one of the basic choices Christians must make to assure their future. The majority of Christian Arabs acknowledge the importance of this dialogue and assign it the highest priority. Even though the old language of polemic is still current in Christian conservative and fundamentalist circles, the historic churches have chosen to close the chapter of past attacks and, in place of this, are engaging in theological efforts that are reopening their own patristic and scriptural heritage. For Christians to get to know Islam has nothing to do with supremacy, or with converting Muslims to Christianity. It is recognition of human, national, and spiritual kinship.

Even so, Christian-Muslim dialogue is strewn with hazards. For example, it is not easy for those engaged in dialogue to remain open to understanding one another without succumbing to the urge to lecture the other. It is difficult not to be governed in one's attitude by the pressures of immediate circumstances. It is difficult for each person to keep a balanced view of the other's religion, avoiding an emphasis on differences and concluding that no consensus is possible. The reverse also is crucial: to avoid glossing over real differences to the point of denying that they exist.

In the present context, filled as it is with tension and the claims of competing fundamentalisms, it is difficult to assess the value of dialogue. It sometimes seems easier completely to abstract it from its political and social incarnation or define it by politics and exploit it for worldly ends and short-term benefits.

3. The "Church of the Arabs"

The future of Christians in the Arab world is bound up with the future of their church. This region is the cradle of religions, and structurally the churches have continued to increase in number so that variety has become division and sectarianism more than a contribution to a rich spiritual heritage. The issue of Christian unity is urgent, but the collective conscience must perceive unity as an imperative both of the gospel and of society. The call to build the "Church of the Arabs" is a call to transcend short-term strategic considerations and look to the future.[3]

To advocate the idea of the "Church of the Arabs" is not to overlook the Armenians, Greeks, Iranians, and others who live in the Middle East Arab world but are beyond the reach of Arab nationalism and language. The "Church of the Arabs" refers rather to "Arabness," which is not limited to a particular ethnicity nor defined by specific religion.

3. Jean Corbon, *L'Eglise des Arabs* (Paris: Cerf, 1997).

The idea behind the "Church of the Arabs" is to incarnate the Christian faith through a sense of belonging to Arab culture, identifying with people, societies, language, culture, and a common destiny.

The "Church of the Arabs" is meant to be a unity in diversity. It is a communion of faith and life. Its faith is one even though the languages of expression and modes of worship may vary. It is a living unity expressing common roots in a single land. This expression of unity already exists — at least to some extent — in and through the Middle East Council of Churches.

4. Owning One's Citizenship

As Christians seek internal renewal and dialogue with Muslims, they raise the spiritual pillars for the integration of Christians into the Arab world, an environment dominated by Muslims. The basic item on their agenda is to discuss how to build a civil society within which all citizens may find opportunity and freedom to engage creatively in building a common future. As they do this, Christians will find that their Muslim interlocutors are tackling a long-deferred agenda of their own — that of working out in Islamic terms a new social contract to replace the medieval one that no longer applies in the modern world.

Owning one's citizenship means that Christians must radically reassess their cultural standards. Openness to Western culture, to modernity, and even to internationalism must not mean the denial of national culture. And, if Christians can extricate themselves from the trials of escapism, from the minority complex, and from alienation, their first priority must be to integrate fully into society. Integration means sinking roots down; it also means active identification with the issues of society.

Christians cannot be saved alone; either the Christians and the Muslims will be saved together, or both will be destroyed. Then and only then will Christians in the Arab world have the right to demand equality — an equality of belonging to a homeland, an equality as citizens. Then Christians will not be anxious about their destiny within the Arab world. Their worry will be for the future of the Arab world, Christian and Muslim together, a future of good and blessing, a future of justice and peace.

The Churches of the Middle East
Now Work Together

Historical Background

It is difficult to pinpoint when the search began in the Middle East for reconciliation among the strands of the unraveled church. For centuries the deep divisions that weakened the churches' common witness had troubled many sensitive Christians.

In 1902 the Ecumenical Patriarch, Yoachim III, issued an encyclical letter from his see in Constantinople. He raised the issues of Christian unity in general and of Orthodox relations with Roman Catholics and Protestants in particular. Eighteen years later a second encyclical was addressed "Unto the Churches of Christ Everywhere." Quoting 1 Peter 1:22, "Love one another earnestly from the heart," the encyclical encouraged the spirit of reconciliation. From that highest seat of Greek Orthodoxy, Patriarch Yoachim echoed the longing in many parts of the Middle East by calling on Christian brothers and sisters to set aside acrimony and contention and to seek those things that make for peace.

A similar mood was developing at that time among the younger churches of the West, whose vision had been broadened through international missionary engagements. Three complementary movements — the International Missionary Council, Faith and Order, and Life and Work —

The authors acknowledge many sources for this chapter, especially within the Middle East Council of Churches. They are especially grateful to Lewis R. Scudder Jr., who has written, edited, or translated many of the Council documents that are available in English.

challenged Western Protestants following historic meetings in Edinburgh and Stockholm. The principal Protestant churches committed themselves to work toward unity and reconciliation, an undertaking that matured in 1948 with the formation of the World Council of Churches.

Even before the 1910 Edinburgh International Missionary Conference, Protestant missions in the Middle East had been seeking ways to relate more closely to each other. Then, in 1924, missionaries met in Jerusalem and organized two United Missionary Councils that became the foundation for the Near East Christian Council. Formed in 1956, the NECC eventually coordinated the efforts of thirty-six Christian agencies and involved the local churches in full partnership. During that period missionary paternalism yielded to a more profound understanding of the church and its witness. By 1962 the mission agencies stepped aside and encouraged the profound transformation of the Near East Christian Council into the Near East Council of Churches.

Within the region, friendly contacts between and among Protestant, Oriental Orthodox, and Eastern Orthodox churches had begun in the 1930s. Significant healing, however, was needed to overcome decades of exploitation, competition, and tension. A concern for reconciliation long expressed within Orthodox spirituality helped in the healing process. These informal efforts led to intentional dialogue in 1964 and to initial planning in 1972 for a more broadly based ecumenical council in the region.

The Second Vatican Council, which began in 1962 during the papacy of Pope John XXIII and concluded under the leadership of Pope Paul VI in 1965, had a profound impact not only on the expression of ecumenism among Catholics but also on Protestant and Orthodox Christians, by stimulating them to seek wider avenues for theological dialogue and practical collaboration.

The first general assembly of the Middle East Council of Churches was held in Nicosia, Cyprus, in May 1974. It was an event of major ecumenical significance, bringing the Eastern Orthodox, Oriental Orthodox, and Evangelical[1] churches together as three families in one council. From the outset, Catholic observers were present as the MECC increasingly expressed and embodied an inclusive approach to ecumenism. In

---

1. In the Middle East, "Evangelical churches" refers to the Protestant churches. See the chapter entitled "The Evangelical (Protestant) Family" for background information.

1984, Catholic prelates joined Orthodox and Protestant leaders in issuing the landmark "Pastoral Epistle of the Heads of Churches in the Middle East." Then, after much careful negotiation, the seven Catholic churches of the Middle East joined the council in 1990 as its fourth family.

Nowhere in the world is there an ecumenical body as inclusive as the MECC, but the reconciliation of the churches in the region is still incomplete. For example, the Ancient Assyrian Church of the East, a strong Christian presence in Iraq, has yet to become fully a part of the MECC. In addition, dialogue continues with several small Protestant churches in the region that have links to non-conciliar Western churches and mission agencies. Increasingly friendly contacts include the partner agencies of some of these churches.

Beyond their participation in the life and activities of the MECC, the churches recognize the need to bridge the theological and liturgical chasms that developed following the great schisms dating back to the fifth century. Their regional efforts parallel and sometimes lead global approaches to overcome these ancient differences.

Contemporary Ministries

Building on their own experience and history, and responding to their own needs and those of the region, the churches of the Middle East Council of Churches have identified five themes or priorities for their common work:

1. *The MECC is committed to strengthening a sense of unity, confidence, continuity, and purpose within the fellowships of its member churches.* The activities and programs of the council seek to encourage Christians to remain in the region and to make positive contributions toward its new and better future.

Significant efforts have been undertaken by the council's Unit on Faith and Unity to help meet those goals. For example, the materials prepared each year for the Week of Prayer for Christian Unity not only have encouraged church members to worship together but also have helped laypersons value their own religious traditions and appreciate the traditions of their neighbors.

In addition, the unit has worked with patience and determination to help the Christian communities in the region agree on a common date for Easter celebrations. Living as minorities throughout the Middle East, Christians understand the weakness of division, especially in relation to their most prominent festivals. The council's leadership in relation to a common date for Easter is reflected beyond the region as well. The MECC co-hosted a global consultation in Aleppo, Syria, with the World Council of Churches on this subject. Orthodox, Catholic, and Protestant groups throughout the world look forward to the time when they can celebrate the resurrection together.

The Unit on Faith and Unity also has developed common Arabic translations of the Lord's Prayer and the Nicene Creed. These have been submitted to the churches through the MECC Executive Committee and are already being used in ecumenical worship.

Other units of the council are seeking to develop a stronger sense of unity and confidence as one basis for reducing the number of Christians emigrating from the region. A major strategy has involved work with young people and young adults. Under the leadership of the Unit on Education and Renewal, youth conferences have been held in Cyprus, Jordan, Syria, and Egypt. Emigration, along with unemployment and issues concerning marriage, are discussed. The ecumenical youth committee in Damascus also organizes ecumenical recitals and international work camps.

2. *The MECC encourages its member churches to support and uphold each other as they help their people understand their faith and witness.* Within the MECC, Christian dialogue takes place on all levels, from the pastoral grass roots to academic halls, from formal dialogue among church leaders to the day-to-day fellowship among Christians on the street. With greater maturity, Christians respond to the demands of their faith and witness.

The Middle East Council of Churches is not only the most inclusive ecumenical body in the world, drawing together as it does Christians from all four of the great families of churches, but it also functions in the region where the Christian faith was born. This means that each of the member churches has its own long history and tradition. Sometimes, in the past, those histories and traditions reflected tensions and divisions within the Body of Christ. One of the principal and urgent goals of the MECC is to encourage the churches to overcome their differences and to bridge the chasms that have separated them from one another. Each of the units and departments of the council develops programs of witness, education, and service, seeking to assist the member churches to engage each other in dialogue and aid each other in practical ways.

Because past differences sprang from or led to theological divergences, ecumenical progress still needs to be made in the area of theology and faith. The Unit on Faith and Unity, for example, has encouraged the various theological faculties in the region to develop more ecumenical approaches by reviewing their curricula and their practices. Meetings have been held for professors of ecumenics and comparative religion. Since 1978 the Association of Theological Institutes in the Middle East (ATIME) has functioned as an affiliate of the MECC. The association seeks to encourage cooperation among the various seminaries and institutes, and among their faculties and students, through conferences, publications, and region-wide student gatherings.

The churches have asked the council to assist them in analyzing and developing their own educational programs in the light of the multi-faith context in which they function. Along with publications in Arabic, French, and English, education is seen by the churches and the council as important to overcoming the weakness of division. The MECC places high priority on reaching youth and young adults by improving family education and counseling, leadership training for teachers and administrators of church-related day schools, activities to help youth function as Christians in a multi-religious society, and study seminars on the changing roles of women in Middle Eastern churches and society. In addition, the MECC seeks to identify scholarship resources for promising young people and future leaders.

A major initiative has been the development of a network of sixteen youth organizations and movements that serve the member churches. Shared priorities for these movements include education for peace and nonviolence, the dialogue between cultures, and the search for justice and human rights.

Workshops for parish clergy have also been held in several countries where member churches are located. Participants share pastoral experiences and concerns and reflect on theological and ecumenical topics. The trust developed in this way leads to increasing collaboration among the parishes of different church bodies. Ecumenical committees have been developed in several countries so that regional emphases can be pursued locally. But the planners of these workshops have come to understand that bishops and other church leaders often need to know more about these conversations among their clergy.

3. *The MECC builds bridges of understanding and mutual respect between Christians and people of other faiths.* The council believes that Christians have a vital role to play within the Middle East's pluralistic society. Although numerically small, a self-confident Christian community knows how to respect and celebrate diversity. The MECC is therefore well positioned to be a bridge between people of different faiths.

One of the most pervasive questions among the churches of the Middle East involves their relations with Muslims and Jews. In every country in the region, Christians need to make their witness in the presence of a dominant and sometimes aggressive Muslim majority. In Israel/Palestine Christians find themselves a "double minority," where Jews as well as Muslims vastly outnumber them. The council's high priority on continuing a dialogue between Christians and Muslims has succeeded in breaking down stereotypes about both religions.

The council's former general secretary, the Reverend Dr. Riad Jarjour, believes that the Muslim-Christian dialogue will raise not only the level of spiritual integration in the Arab world but also the level of involvement by Arab Christians within their societies. "Full social participation presupposes moving from sharing to realizing full equality on the level of citizenship," he says. While many church leaders have participated in the dialogues, the general secretary himself has coordinated the council's involvement in this area. He believes that "without a doubt the dialogues have stimulated optimism and improved understanding between Christians and Muslims."

4. *The MECC nurtures within the churches the spirit and resources for service* (diakonia). The Middle East is an arena for economic and political conflict, often violent conflict. In this environment the legions of

the poor, the downtrodden and exploited, the sick and the suffering, the deprived, disenfranchised, and displaced grow more numerous every day. What guides the council in its ministry of compassion and service is the realization that Christ died for *all* people. To heal, to transcend barriers, and to touch not only the spiritual but the material, social, and physical needs of people is to imitate Christ.

The member churches of the MECC work together through the council's Unit on Life and Service to coordinate their diaconal ministries, especially in development and service to the poor and marginalized, to refugees and migrants. In response to the continuing conflicts in the region, many Christian institutions are involved in these service ministries; by collaborating through this unit they are able to avoid competition and to complement each other.

Through their council, the churches have affirmed that Christian involvement in social service is "legitimate, important and urgent." In official documents they call such *diakonia* "Eucharist in action," an expression that springs from the *koinonia* (fellowship) of the church. They also have affirmed that this social witness can most appropriately be done ecumenically.

"*Diakonia* is more than charity," the former director of the unit, Aline Papazian, insists. "It is an expression of love through sharing, and an affirmation that in justice human dignity is sustained." Because the council believes that the spiritual dimension of this sharing is so important, the unit places high priority on its training programs and educational activities, so that a "spirituality of social action" can be developed.

A region-wide health program has assessed the specific health issues and challenges facing the Middle Eastern societies. By linking the church-related health institutions, the sharing of information, skills, and experiences is possible. The program has been responsible for surveys, health training seminars, and the publication of urgently needed materials. It has also facilitated the sharing of human resources among the related health institutions.

5. *The MECC is a mediator not only between Christians and churches in the Middle East but also between them and their brothers and sisters in Christ elsewhere.* Social and cultural gaps often impede or undermine un-

derstanding; but with its historical heritage, the council is uniquely equipped to bridge these gaps, to nurture trust in partner relationships, and to focus broad Christian concern for justice, peace, and the relief of human suffering in the region.

Churches and mission agencies in western Europe, North America, and Australia have long been involved in the region. These mission agencies have moved from direct involvement "on the ground" to a stance of support, partnership, and solidarity with the indigenous churches. One indication of the ecumenical posture of these agencies is that wherever possible they prefer to work in partnership through the Middle East Council of Churches.

Each of the council's units enjoys such partnership relations. In addition, the council coordinates three separately funded and administered programs on behalf of the partners. One of these, the Department of Service to Palestinian Refugees (DSPR), maintains a wide range of services from health care to vocational training in Gaza, the West Bank, Galilee, Jordan, and Lebanon. Ever since the 1940s, this department has helped refugees express their needs and develop their potential. Direct aid and assistance has played a major role in this ministry, but the DSPR also serves as a strong advocate of Palestinian rights and their hopes for peace. The programs in the five areas are directed locally and supervised from Jerusalem by the executive director, Professor Bernard Sabella.

Another program, known as Ecumenical Relief Services (ERS), currently provides essential relief services in Iraq because of the human crisis of massive proportions. Problems include malnutrition (especially among children), increased physical and psychological trauma, and the near collapse of the nation's health care system. The MECC's field coordinator manages the relief efforts of the partner agencies in the United States and Canada, Sweden, and Denmark, and through "Action by Churches Together" (ACT), an organization related to the World Council of Churches. Most of the medical support given through ERS is provided at the request of the Ministry of Health. Recently medicine, orthopedic supplies, syringes, gloves, and other supplies were distributed to hospitals in all Iraqi governorates.

The third program is involved in emergency relief, rehabilitation, and reconstruction in Lebanon. This program, formerly known as

ERR, was launched in 1975 to help the Lebanese churches cope with the effects of the civil war and to enable them to assist its victims. Now known as the Inter-Church Network for Development and Relief in Lebanon, the program involves training, educational assistance, the development of income-generating projects, and community health and rural development programs. ICNDR has assisted in the reconstruction of private homes, churches, community institutions, and infrastructure. Training for local initiatives was a high priority of the director, Ms. Souad Hajj Nassif, especially following the withdrawal of the Israeli army from its twenty-two-year occupation of a strip of land representing 15 percent of Lebanon's total area. The area had a population of more than half a million persons.

In varying ways the units also have given issues of justice, peace, and human rights a high priority in their activities. Among other efforts, training in human rights advocacy was provided to the churches and key lay members. A seminar on "Violence Against Women in the Middle East" was co-sponsored by the MECC and the World Council of Churches, and one on the problems of "Young People in Situations of Conflict" was a joint venture with the Ayia Napa Conference Center in Cyprus. In addition, a seminar on conflict resolution was held.

MECC Organization

The Middle East Council of Churches has provided programmatic responses to the five priorities, even though priorities may involve more than one part of the council's organization.

Because the council *is* the member churches at work together, the churches determine the life and direction of the MECC's work. To provide a coherent and effective pattern for their work, the member churches function within the council through the four families of churches. The general assembly, which sets policy for the whole of the council, is made up of twenty-four delegates from each family. The general assembly typically meets every four years.

There also are four presidents, one from each family. The presidents carry a broad range of responsibilities, including presiding in turn over sessions of the general assembly and the executive committee. Because of their ecclesiastical stature in the region and beyond, they frequently represent the council and provide counsel to the general secretary and the staff. Each of the families of churches also is represented on the executive committee. This committee meets at least once a year.

In recent years the MECC has faced the challenge of shrinking resources. Although this has forced a reduction in staff and fewer meetings, the council seeks to maintain its broad purposes and continues to engage its member churches across a wide and often very tense region.

In addition to political tensions, there are sometimes issues between the member churches of the Council. As this edition was going to press, reports were circulating about a rift between the Patriarch of the Coptic Orthodox Church and the Jerusalem Patriarch of the Greek Orthodox Church. Since both have held presidencies in the Middle East Council of Churches, many concerned persons were eager to have the controversy settled without doing permanent damage.

The MECC's headquarters are in Beirut, Lebanon. It also maintains a presence in Cairo, Egypt; Amman, Jordan; Dubai, United Arab Emirates; and Jerusalem. The general secretary may be reached at MECC, Deeb Building, Makhoul Street, P.O. Box 5376, Beirut, Lebanon; Tel: +961.1.353.938; Fax: +961.1.344.894; E-mail: guirgissaleh@cyberia.net.lb; website: www.mec-churches.org.

The Importance of Jerusalem to Christians

All over the world, Catholic churches have a piece of Jerusalem within them known as the Stations of the Cross. This architectural feature began as a way of allowing Christians to follow the Via Dolorosa even when they were not able to travel to Jerusalem, and of helping those who had visited the Holy Land to remember Jerusalem when they returned home. Orthodox churches have direct references to Jerusalem in their liturgies, especially during Holy Week. They hold the city sacred. Protestants often say, quoting Jesus, that worship is to be "in spirit and in truth" rather than at any one place. The playing down of holy sites began when Luther discouraged pilgrimage as a way to earn indulgences. Nevertheless, many Protestant churches have pictures or stained glass windows that contain scenes of Jerusalem. References to Jerusalem, Zion, and the Holy City are common in hymns and anthems.

After the crucifixion and resurrection of Jesus, the church was born in Jerusalem on Pentecost. Even though the Christians were persecuted by the Jewish authorities, the "mother of all churches" was in Jerusalem and it was the place to which apostles returned and in which councils were held. In A.D. 70 when the Romans turned Jerusalem into a pagan city, they changed its name to Aelia Capitolina. Still, Christians filtered back in, and once Emperor Constantine declared Christianity a legal religion in the Roman Empire in the fourth century, Jerusalem became the center of Christian spirituality and pilgrimage. As the church grew, Jerusalem was venerated, but its churches and institutions were governed by patriarchs and bishops who lived elsewhere.

Pilgrims journeyed to Jerusalem from the whole Mediterranean basin and even further. Some decided to stay and founded hostels for other pilgrims from their ethnic group. Others stayed to become monks and nuns. Some monks started monasteries; others became hermits in the desert just east of Jerusalem. All spiritual roads seemed to lead to Jerusalem rather than to Rome. In 451 Jerusalem became a patriarchate, an acknowledgment of the city's importance to Christianity.

From 614 to 628 the Persians demolished all the Christian churches, sparing only the Church of the Nativity (see p. 161) in Bethlehem and weakening the Christian hold on Jerusalem. In 638 when the Patriarch Sophronius surrendered the city to the Muslim Caliph Omar, he handed over the keys to the city sadly but peacefully. In deference to Christianity, the Caliph declined to pray in the Church of the Holy Sepulchre so that Muslims would not claim it as a mosque. Omar also issued an edict that gave both Christians and Jews access to their holy sites and freedom of worship.

During the Middle Ages Jerusalem was considered the center of the world by Christians. A famous map of the three continents of Africa, Asia, and Europe shows Jerusalem as the center from which the continents radiate. Even today, the Greek Orthodox call their cathedral in the Church of the Resurrection (Church of the Holy Sepulchre) the *Catholican* (universal site) and mark a spot, known as the *omphalos* (the navel), as the center of the earth.

It is said that Christians of Jerusalem have long religious memories, still remembering the Crusades and the devastation they brought to the church of Jerusalem. The crusaders were motivated by many things — economic, political, and religious — but part of their goal was to redevelop the pilgrimage routes to Jerusalem for the use of Catholic pilgrims. Even after the crusaders were defeated by Islamic forces, Jerusalem remained an important Christian city. The city reverted to its Orthodox patriarch, but after 1333 Franciscan friars were sent by the pope to guard the religious sites along with guardians from the Orthodox and Armenian patriarchates.

As part of the Ottoman Empire, Jerusalem retained its character as a city of Christians, Jews, and Muslims. Christians had their ups and downs, but by the late nineteenth century Western groups arrived as "protectors" of the Christian communities. Every country wanted a presence in Jerusalem, and today there are areas known as the German

Colony and the American Colony (where a hotel by that name still stands). There is a hospital with an Italianate building, and a French hotel known as Notre Dame. The church in the Austrian Hospice looks as though it had been moved piece by piece from Vienna.

After the fall of the Ottoman Empire the British were given the mandate to help Palestine become an independent country. As a result of heavy Jewish immigration, however, they threw up their hands and asked the United Nations to partition the area. UN Resolution 181 divided the land and included a *Corpus Separatum* for Greater Jerusalem, including Bethlehem, recognizing the international and interreligious character of the city. From the 1948 war to the 1967 war, the city was part Israeli and part Jordanian.

The Oslo Accords delayed the resolution of the issue of Jerusalem, and Israel today claims the entire city, despite international laws that prohibit the acquisition of land by occupation. The Israeli government is seeking to further its goals through demographic changes by denying building permits to non-Jews and by confiscating IDs and taking over pieces of land from Christians and Muslims. Christian residents still remember when Jewish settlers seized St. John's Hospice, located at the entrance to the Church of the Holy Sepulchre, in 1990. Since the takeover happened during Holy Week Christians were extremely upset and closed all the churches for a twenty-four-hour period, tolling their bells as if at a funeral.

Christians have been emigrating from the city and the area, leaving a dwindling number of believers in the midst of Jews and Muslims. Concern has been voiced for years that Jerusalem, the center of Christianity, could become more like a museum than a living Christian community. At this writing local Christians who do not have Jerusalem IDs cannot visit the holy sites and several Christian institutions have been threatened with seizure by the collection of back taxes from which they had been exempt. Housing in Jerusalem is very expensive and Jews are given special allowances by the government to enable them to live in Jerusalem while Christians have no help with expenses. This is the first time since A.D. 70 that Christians are a minority under a Jewish majority.

Although the church is universal, Jerusalem is its spiritual homeland — the spiritual capital for all Christians. Jerusalem has an important place in the origin of Christianity both as the place of Jesus' death and resurrection and as the founding location of the church. In Christian theology, salvation took place here. Christians believe in an incarnate God and believe that salvation happened in a particular time and place. Jerusalem is that place. To the local Christians (and to Muslims) it is known as *Al-Quds,* which is Arabic for "The Holy," and the city itself is considered a witness to the resurrection.

There has been a nearly continuous Christian presence in Jerusalem since the beginning of the church. Without the people the holy sites die and become symbols of an ancient religion rather than a living faith. Attempts by tour agencies to encourage Christians to visit only sites and not people have been detrimental to the churches of Jerusalem as well as to the unity of Christianity. With the development of mass tourism, which leads people to admire the buildings rather than meet the people, the attachment to Jerusalem has dwindled around the world. This disconnect has been experienced particularly by Christians outside the Holy Land who tend to look on the faith as Western rather than universal.

In the early years of pilgrimage, Jerusalem was the primary goal and the city from which liturgical customs emanated. Rites and rituals were begun there and pilgrims went to meet the living stones as well as to be in the presence of the ancient stones. Until recently rituals such as the procession down the Mount of Olives on Palm Sunday, the lighting of the holy fire in the Church of the Holy Sepulchre on Easter Saturday, and the pilgrimage to the Field of the Shepherds in Beit Sahour and the grotto in Bethlehem were part of the life of the local people. Now checkpoints, walls, and permits prohibit indigenous Christians from partaking in the ancient rituals. Freedom to worship is dwindling for them and, therefore, for all Christians. The extinction of living Christianity in Jerusalem should be a concern for people everywhere.

The Christians of Jerusalem have been the living stones connecting ethnic groups and denominations with one another (though not always peacefully). No division in the church universal began in Jerusalem, although with groups vying for closeness to "Mother Church" there has been jealousy and strain. But when the suggestion was made in 2001 that Israel should control the Jewish and Armenian quarters and the Palestinians control the Christian and Muslim quarters, the whole Christian community presented a united front in demanding that all Christian groups remain united.

Christianity is important to Jerusalem just as Jerusalem is important to Christianity. Jerusalem's place as a spiritual center has meant
that Christians from around the world have started hospitals, schools,
and social concern institutions. Centers for study and theological research have been set up in the city and archeological institutes have
been built by several countries, often under Christian sponsorship.
Some of these institutions are being threatened today by laws that
limit access and outside funding and by Israeli taxes that could bank-
rupt them.

The enmity that has grown between Israel and the Arabs (both
Muslims and Christians) spills over to an enmity between Muslims and
Jews in Jerusalem and in other parts of the world. This is true despite
the many centuries in which the Muslim world held Judaism in greater
regard than the Christian world did. (For example, in 1492, when expelled from Spain by the Christians, Jews fled to Muslim countries
rather than to other Christian countries.)

Beginning in Jerusalem, Christians in general and Arab Christians
in particular are seeing their role as one of reconciliation in situations
of conflict and as a force for justice and peace in a land that is holy to
three faiths.

A Timeline of Christianity in the Middle East

Date	Event
33	– Pentecost
36	– Saul converted on road to Damascus
37-43	– Peter establishes church in Antioch, where for the first time the disciples are called Christians (Acts 11:26)
61-64	– Mark founds the Christian church in Egypt
68	– Mark is martyred in Alexandria
70	– Jerusalem temple destroyed by Romans; Christians flee to Pella temporarily before filtering back into Jerusalem
135	– Jerusalem destroyed by Hadrian and Aelia Capitolina built on ruins
200	– Septimus Severus issues edict against Christians
284	– Beginning of reign of Diocletian
	– "Anno Martyri"; Copts begin their calendar with this year
285	– St. Anthony becomes hermit in Egypt
303	– Armenia becomes Christian when King Tiridates III is converted by Gregory the Illuminator
	– Edict of Diocletian begins bloodiest persecutions
313	– Edict of Toleration (Edict of Milan) grants Christianity the legal right to exist
314	– Emperor Constantine embraces Christianity
317	– Monastic life, as different from hermit life, initiated by Pachomius in Upper Egypt
325	– First Ecumenical Council meets in Nicea:

	– Athenasius debates Arius, who is denounced as a heretic
	– Method of calculating the date of Easter agreed upon
330	– Inauguration of Constantinople as the New Rome by Emperor Constantine
365	– Armenian Church declares complete independence from Constantinople
380	– Christianity is declared religion of Roman Empire by decree of Theodosius
381	– Second Ecumenical Council meets in Constantinople: – Constantinople recognized as a patriarchate
382	– Nicene Creed adopted
392-404	– Mesrob creates Armenian alphabet and translates Bible
395	– Division of Roman Empire into East and West
431	– Third Ecumenical Council meets in Ephesus: – Nestorius is condemned as heretic – Church of Cyprus recognized as autocephalous
451	– Fourth Ecumenical Council meets in Chalcedon: – Council recognizes two natures of Christ inseparable in one person – Patriarchates of Antioch and Alexandria are both split by decision – Patriarchate of Jerusalem formed
486	– Council of Seleucia held: – Church of Persia ends tie to Antioch; rejects findings of Council of Ephesus in 431 concerning Nestorius
520	– Patriarch of Constantinople given title Ecumenical Patriarch – Church of Armenia excommunicates Constantinople
543	– Yacub (Jacob) al Baradai consecrated Bishop of Edessa; revives liturgical life of Syriac (Syrian) Orthodox Church
551	– Armenian Church formally rejects teaching of Council of Chalcedon
553	– Fifth Ecumenical Council meets in Constantinople
571	– Birth of the Prophet Muhammad
614	– Persians occupy Jerusalem and destroy Christian religious sites
622	– Hijra: Prophet Muhammad leaves Mecca for Medina: – Muslim calendar is dated from this year

632	– Death of the Prophet Muhammad
638	– Antioch and Jerusalem surrender to Caliph Omar
	– Syrian, Greek, and Armenian Patriarchates are relocated from Antioch
680	– Sixth Ecumenical Council meets in Constantinople
	– Separation of Greek and Syriac Orthodox Patriarchates in Antioch
685	– Monks of St. Maron elect John Maron as patriarch
710	– Maronite Church becomes autonomous
787	– Seventh Ecumenical Council meets in Nicea:
	– Icons affirmed as objects of reverence
988	– Prince Vladimir of Kiev and his people are baptized
1054	– Schism between Constantinople and Rome with mutual excommunications
1096	– Antioch falls to crusaders
1099	– Jerusalem falls to crusaders
	– Latin Patriarchate is established in Jerusalem
1187	– Crusaders abandon Jerusalem after defeat by Salah al-Din (Saladin) at Horns of Hittin
1204	– Fourth Crusade seizes and sacks Constantinople
1366	– Damascus becomes seat of Greek Orthodox Patriarch of Antioch
1453	– Constantinople falls to Ottomans; Greek Orthodox Patriarchate is recognized as the civil authority for Christians
1517	– Syria, Egypt, and Palestine fall to Ottomans
	– Martin Luther posts Ninety-Five Theses on door of Wittenberg church
1553	– Pope recognizes Simon VIII as patriarch of Chaldeans
1729	– Greek Catholics (Melkites) recognized by Vatican
1740	– Cyril VI given title of Greek Catholic Patriarch
1742	– Rome recognizes Armenian Catholic Patriarch Abraham Pierre I
1798	– Napoleon invades Egypt
1823	– Arrival of first Congregational and Presbyterian missionaries in Beirut
1832	– First Evangelical (Episcopal) church in Iran

1841	– British Anglicans and German Lutherans found joint bishopric in Holy Land
1846	– Organization of first Armenian Evangelical church in Istanbul
1847	– Pope Pius IX reestablishes Latin Patriarchate in Jerusalem
1848	– Organization of first Arab-speaking Evangelical church in Middle East in Beirut
1850	– Formal recognition of first Protestant *millet*
1852	– Ottoman declaration of the formal Status Quo of holy sites in Jerusalem and Bethlehem
1863	– Evangelical Church in Egypt formed following creation of schools by American Presbyterians
1882	– British occupy Egypt and by 1898 also control Sudan
1892	– Greek Orthodox Patriarchate of Antioch names first Arab patriarch
1902	– Ecumenical Patriarch Yoachim III issues encyclical urging Orthodox Christians to "seek points of encounter" with other churches
1910	– Edinburgh International Missionary Conference held, which leads to Protestant and Orthodox ecumenical councils
1915-22	– Armenian genocide
1917	– Fall of Ottoman Empire
	– British sign Balfour Declaration providing political sanction for "a national home for the Jewish people in Palestine"
1920	– Ecumenical Patriarchate calls for all churches to form a "communion" of churches
	– League of Nations partitions Greater Syria; provides mandates to French (Syria and Lebanon) and British (Palestine, Transjordan, and Iraq)
1923	– Union of Armenian Evangelical Churches established in Beirut
1924	– United Missionary Council founded in Jerusalem
1943	– Lebanon becomes independent (from French mandate)
1944	– Syria becomes independent (from French mandate)
1946	– Jordan becomes independent (from British mandate)
1947	– UN Resolution 181 partitions Palestine

1948   – British end mandate in Palestine, UN partition of Palestine fails, and State of Israel proclaims its independence
           – World Council of Churches holds first Assembly in Amsterdam

1953   – Egypt becomes a republic

1956   – Near East Christian Council founded

1958   – Evangelical Church in Egypt becomes independent from the Presbyterian mission
           – Coptic Evangelical Organization for Social Services (CEOSS) formed

1959   – National Evangelical Synod of Syria and Lebanon formed as successor to Presbyterian mission

1961   – Orthodox churches from Eastern Europe's communist bloc join World Council of Churches at New Delhi Assembly
           – Ecumenical Bureau for Youth and Students in Middle East opened in Beirut

1962-65   – Vatican II held in Rome, "modernizing" the Roman Catholic Church:
             – Eastern Catholic churches given greater leeway in using traditional liturgies

1962   – Near East Council of Churches founded

1964   – Pope Paul VI and Ecumenical Patriarch Athenagoras I meet in Jerusalem, repeal mutual anathemas; in 1965 they annul mutual excommunication of 1054

1965   – Synod of non-Chalcedonian Churches in Addis Ababa
           – National Evangelical Union of Lebanon formed

1968   – Pope Paul VI returns relics of St. Mark to Coptic Pope Kyrillos VI

1973   – Pope Shenouda III of Coptic Orthodox Church meets Pope Paul VI of Catholic Church; they sign declaration of confession of one and the same faith

1974   – Middle East Council of Churches (replacing the Near East Council of Churches) holds its first assembly in Nicosia, Cyprus; three families of churches are members: Eastern Orthodox, Oriental Orthodox, and Evangelical
           – Fellowship of the Middle East Evangelical Churches (FMEEC) holds its first general assembly

1984   – Pope John Paul II and Syriac Patriarch Ignace Zakka I Iwas sign declaration of confession of one and the same faith

1990   – Catholic family of churches joins MECC at fifth general assembly as fourth family of churches

1994   – Pope John Paul II and Mar Dinkha IV, Patriarch of the Assyrian Church of the East, sign historic "Common Christological Declaration" ending isolation dating from Council of Ephesus in 431

1996   – Pope John Paul II and Armenian Catholicos Karekin I sign declaration of confession of one and the same faith

1997   – Restoration of the Church of the Holy Sepulchre in Jerusalem

1998   – MECC and WCC sponsor meeting in Aleppo, Syria, seeking the basis for a common date for Easter; the gathering was hosted by the Syriac Orthodox Church
      – Oriental Orthodox meet to reaffirm their unity in faith

2002   – On January 21 Jewish, Islamic, and Christian religious leaders in the Middle East adopted the Alexandria Declaration that recognizes the sanctity of the Holy Land for all three faiths and calls for an end to "the violence and bloodshed"

2004   – Ecumenical Patriarch Bartholomew I accepts an apology offered by Pope John Paul II in 2001, for the sacking of Constantinople in 1204

2006   – Evangelical churches sign an "Agreement of Full Mutual Recognition Between the Lutheran and Reformed Churches in the Middle East and North Africa"
      – Ecumenical Patriarch Bartholomew I and Pope Benedict XVI meet in Istanbul and affirm their commitment to work toward the restoration of full communion

2007   – On May 18 at a ceremony in Moscow's Cathedral of Christ the Savior, the Russian Orthodox Church and the Russian Orthodox Church Outside of Russia (sometimes known as the white Russians) officially end a division that began in 1927
      – On June 18-20 in Amman, Jordan, at a meeting sponsored by the World Council of Churches, representatives of

churches and church-related organizations launch the
Palestine Israel Ecumenical Forum

– On July 13 in Cairo the Coptic Orthodox Church and the
Ethiopian Orthodox *Tewahedo* Church "solemnly declare
their unity of faith, their commitment to a common
witness and their readiness to deepen and expand
collaboration"

2008   – On September 10-14 in Bern, Switzerland, theologians
and church representatives reflect on issues such as the
"Promised Land," "the Church and Israel," and "Justice
and Peace." This was organized by the World Council of
Churches in the framework of the June 2007 Palestine
Israel Ecumenical Forum

2009   – On May 15 at a consultation at the Ukrainian Catholic
University in Lviv, participants endorse a 1998
compromise on the date of Easter. It would follow the
Nicea rule but calculate the equinox and full moon using
the more accurate astronomical data available today

– In December leaders of the churches in Israel and
Palestine draft The Kairos Palestinian Document calling
for an end to the occupation of Palestine by Israel and
expressing hope as Christians

– A December meeting of the Fellowship of Middle East
Evangelical Churches in Harissa, Lebanon, unanimously
approves the ordination of women as pastors

A Word about Numbers

The numbers used in this book are, at best, only rough estimates.

Theologically, as well as practically, the ancient churches of the Middle East are reserved about membership statistics. For them, history is ever present: they celebrate their origins at the first Pentecost. They view the Western fascination with counting current members as superficial. Amid the icons of the saints, they feel constantly surrounded "by the cloud of witnesses." They also believe that Western Christians too often ignore the promise that the Lord of the church is present "where two or three" gather in Christ's name.

Also, in places where a census is only occasional and is generally imprecise, churches have little or no capacity to count their scattered flock. Family groups are associated with a geographical parish into which individuals are born. They know little of the style of American Protestants who "join" a congregation, often moving from one denomination to another. The churches of the East are far more concerned about correct doctrine than about the size of congregations.

Still, some measurement seems useful, especially in the light of continued anxiety over the emigration of Christians from the region. Therefore, we have attempted to gather such data as is available and to offer conservative estimates. Each of the churches has been requested to provide its most reliable and most recent figures. Statistics furnished by the churches themselves are used when available. Frequently percentages are offered to facilitate broad comparisons and to signal certain trends.

In general it can be noted that Christian families tend to be smaller than their Muslim or Jewish counterparts, and that Protestant families tend to be smaller than those of other Christian groups. For Christians, even modest emigration can result in a serious loss in percentages. Social scientists who study emigration trends appear to agree that those who leave the Middle East seeking educational and economic opportunities generally are from the middle classes — regardless of their religious persuasion. It seems likely that the historical Christian commitment to quality education therefore actually encourages emigration.

Readers seeking exact statistics will be disappointed; they will do well to be skeptical about the numbers presented here.

PART II

PROFILES OF THE CHURCHES

The Origins of the Diversity of Christianity in the Middle East

Christianity has its home in the Middle East with the primitive church of Jerusalem being the Judeo-Christian church founded at Pentecost. As the Judeo-Christian church expanded beyond the synagogues of the Mediterranean basin, it was eclipsed by the Hellenistic (Greek-speaking) church but survived until the end of the fourth century. It still carried the title of the "Mother Church" of Christianity. Today's Eastern churches and Western churches have both grown out of that church begun at Pentecost in Jerusalem and been carried throughout the world primarily through the Hellenistic branch.[1] The Middle East Council of Churches groups today's denominations into four families: Eastern Orthodox, Oriental Orthodox, Catholic, and Evangelical[2] and Anglican.

In the beginning there were no such entities as denominations and the church was one unified body. As it grew rapidly over a large area, there was a need for organization and the church (still unified) was divided into geographical units called patriarchates. The earliest patriarchates were in Antioch, Alexandria, and Rome. By the fifth century there would be patriarchates in Constantinople and Jerusalem as well, with Constantinople designated as the first patriarchate or "first

---

1. Beyond the scope of this book are the churches that spread east to India and China and south into Ethiopia along ancient trade routes. The Apostle Thomas became known as the founder of some of the eastern churches, including the Mar Thoma Church of India. Early Jewish Christians from Ethiopia are honored as the founders of the Orthodox Church there after hearing the teachings of Philip (see Acts 8:28-40.)

2. In the Middle East, "Evangelical churches" refers to the Protestant churches. See the chapter entitled "The Evangelical (Protestant) Family" for background information.

among equals." Although Jerusalem was not a large patriarchate it was honored because it was the "Mother Church."

As the church grew in those early centuries, the Christians suffered both periods of persecutions and challenges of theological differences. The persecutions ended with the Edict of Toleration in 313 but the theological turmoil continued much longer and would become the basis of diverse churches (sometimes called communions or denominations). After establishing a new capital in Byzantium called Constantinople, the Emperor Constantine realized that theological division, which was beginning to occur, could threaten political stability, so he called three hundred bishops to the First Ecumenical Council in Nicea in 325. The statement that Christ was "true God of true God, begotten not made, of one substance with the Father" was articulated at that council and later ratified at the 381 Council of Constantinople as part of the Nicene Creed. It was in 381 that Constantinople became the fourth patriarchate because it was the capital of the empire and sometimes called the Second Rome.

During Constantine's rule the Roman Empire was divided into the Western Roman Empire with its capital in Rome and the Eastern Roman Empire with its capital at Constantinople. As the civil jurisdictions divided so did the church jurisdictions, resulting in a growing political divide in the church between the Eastern Church and the Western Church. It was not until the council at Ephesus in 431, however, that the first significant *theological* break occurred. It was at Ephesus that some Christians declared their belief in the separation of the two natures of Jesus Christ. Many of them found a compatible home in the Church of the East that had already broken off from the official church of the Roman Empire for political reasons. Instead of unity, the result of the ecumenical councils was charges of heresy, divisions in the church, and less political stability.

Although several other councils produced splits in the church, the major split occurred in 451 at Chalcedon when the nature of Christ was stated definitively. Now in addition to the divide between the East and the West, the Eastern Church itself was split. The Oriental Orthodox churches are those who did not accept the theological understanding of the nature of Jesus Christ proclaimed at the Council of Chalcedon, namely, that Christ is one person in two natures "of one substance with the Father according to His divinity, of one substance with us according to His humanity. . . . Only begotten in two natures without confusion, without change, without division, without separation." Some of the Oriental Orthodox churches give greater emphasis to the divine nature of Jesus while others state the nature of Christ by a different formula. In addition to these theological reasons for rejecting the teaching of Chalcedon, the Oriental Orthodox churches also had nontheological reasons. There was much political maneuvering and persecution by the Byzantine (Eastern) church in addition to the theological differences that set the churches apart. As a result of this split, the Oriental Orthodox churches would not be involved in the later ecumenical councils that dealt with the veneration of icons. The Oriental Orthodox family of churches now includes the Armenian Orthodox, the Coptic Orthodox, the Ethiopian Orthodox, and the Syriac Orthodox churches, all of which have remained national religious groups.

Those Orthodox churches that accepted the formulation from the Council at Chalcedon are known as the Eastern Orthodox churches. The principal Eastern Orthodox Church is the Greek Orthodox Church with its Ecumenical Patriarchate in Istanbul (formerly Constantinople). Another Eastern Orthodox Church, with a small number of churches in the Middle East, is the Russian Orthodox Church, formed in 988. It established itself in Jerusalem because of the large numbers of Russian pilgrims. Russian churches in the Holy Land today include both the churches related to the patriarchate in Moscow (the so-called Red Russian) and churches related to the breakaway Russian Orthodox Church Outside Russia (the so-called White Russian), which was formed after the Russian revolution. In 2007 the churches reunited. Recently there have been contacts between Oriental Orthodox churches and Eastern Orthodox churches clarifying issues and confirming that both groups really represent the same faith expressed in different ways.

Even more significant for the Christian church as a whole than this divide between Oriental and Eastern Orthodox churches was the original split between West and East, which continued to grow as political and theological controversies swept over the empire. By the end of the sixth century the Western churches were using Latin while the Eastern churches used Greek, and in addition to the language differences there were a number of ecclesiastical practices that diverged. In the East leavened bread was used in the Eucharist while the West used unleavened bread. The West required celibacy while the Eastern churches allowed some clergy to marry. The Western churches looked to Rome for authority while the Eastern churches acknowledged the Pope as only the first among equals. Theologically the two groups fought over a clause inserted by the Latin Church into the Nicene Creed at a Western ecumenical council in Toledo in 589. Known as the *filioque,* it indicated that the Holy Spirit proceeded from the Father and the Son; the Eastern churches rejected the addition of "and the Son." The year 1054, when the Patriarch of Constantinople and the Roman papal legate excommunicated each other, stands out as the culminating point of the growing schism between what are known as the Eastern Orthodox and the Roman Catholic churches.

Up until that period, the patriarchates in the East and the Roman Patriarchate stayed out of each other's territories even though they were at odds. Only a few years after the major schism, however, the Crusades began and completely terminated the relationship, as the Latin Catholic crusaders slaughtered Orthodox Christians as well as Muslims. The soldiers of the Fourth Crusade ended all hope of reconciliation with the ransacking of the Church of the Holy Wisdom in Constantinople in 1204. Attempts at reunion in the thirteenth and fifteenth centuries failed, although the twentieth century saw progress.

What many know as the Roman Catholic Church is known in the Middle East as the Latin Catholic Church and is the continuation of the Roman Patriarchate. Today's Latin Patriarchate was established in Jerusalem for the first time in 1099 as part of the Crusades when the Orthodox Patriarch was sent into exile. After the crusaders were defeated and the Orthodox Patriarch was restored there was no Latin Patriarch in the Holy Land. The Pope, with the explicit permission of Muslim leaders, made the Franciscan friars the custodians of the churches and shrines in the Holy Land. The Latin Patriarchate was re-established in 1847, but the Franciscans continue in their role as custodians of the holy places.

The Reformation is a Western phenomenon and the Eastern churches never went through a similar crisis. Nevertheless, it did leave its mark on the Eastern churches through the missionary movement of the eighteenth and nineteenth centuries. Part of the missionary movement was targeted at converting Muslims and Jews in the Middle East, but when they did not respond the missionaries turned to converting Eastern Christians. Some Protestant missionaries looked at the Eastern churches as dead churches in need of some new life. Missionary activity to enliven them became an effort to convert Orthodox believers to Western evangelical fervor and to the formation of Evangelical (Protestant) churches in the Middle East.

The Episcopal Church of Jerusalem and the Evangelical Lutheran Church in Jordan and the Holy Land were founded by the Church of England and the German Lutheran Church in the nineteenth century. Methodists worked in North Africa, the Reformed churches in the Gulf, the Congregationalists in Turkey, and the Presbyterians in Egypt, Iran, Sudan, and what became Lebanon and Syria. These churches are under Arab leadership today but have congregations of expatriates as well.

Mostly as a result of missionary activity on the part of the Latin Catholics (Roman Catholics), portions of the Orthodox churches have come into communion with Rome. Parts of the Orthodox patriarchates and the Oriental Orthodox churches have had periods of communion with Rome for centuries, but the establishment of these groups as separate and recognized churches did not occur until the eighteenth century. The Greek Catholic Church (or Melkite Church) was officially founded in 1724 after a split in the Patriarchate of Antioch, but parishes from other patriarchates also became affiliated with it. The Armenian Catholic Patriarchate dates to 1740; the first Syriac Catholic Patriarchate to 1783; and the Coptic Catholic Patriarchate of Alexandria to 1895. Although they are part of the Catholic Church, they still use their ancient Orthodox liturgies and language.

In the Ottoman Empire a number of European countries laid claim to "protecting" various religious groups. The Russians, for instance, became the protectors of the Orthodox while the French backed the Latin Catholics. Since some churches (such as the Armenian Orthodox Church) were of a national origin, they remained tied to their own countries of origin. Political wars played themselves out in religious squabbles. When battles ensued over the holy sites (as much political as religious) the Ottomans promulgated the Status Quo in 1852. This agreement, which has been honored by all governments since then, delineated the spaces in holy sites and the times and places of celebrations allotted to various traditional denominations.

Today's approach is one of mending past schisms and working ecumenically on contemporary problems. This is represented both in councils of churches and by bilateral and multilateral discussions. History has left its mark, but modern circumstances are reversing the years of enmity.

Dhimmi Status and the *Millet* System

Dhimmi is the minority status given to non-Muslims in the Muslim world through much of history. The Jews and Christians were "People of the Book," and therefore were tolerated minorities who owed a tax to the state but did not serve in the army. They often did play a significant role in government, the arts, architecture, and languages.

The Ottoman Empire dealt with non-Muslim *Dhimmis* (as the Jews and Christians were called) through the *millet* system, especially during the nineteenth century. Under the *millet* system, the ranking religious leader was recognized by the government and, in turn, was responsible for relations with the government, including the payment of taxes. He was also responsible for the internal workings of the *millet,* which encompassed much more than the typical functions of a church organization; education and personal law — including marriage, divorce, birth, death, and inheritance — were under the jurisdiction of the head of the church as well.

The *millet* system kept the various Christian groups apart from one another and reduced friction. It also led to much greater self-consciousness in the churches and discouraged conversion from one to another. By the twentieth century, individual *millets* had come under the protection of foreign governments. Equality with Muslim citizens and the elimination of the *millet* system caused tension in the empire during the period of nationalism and pan-Arabism.

There are still vestiges of the *millet* system in Syria, Lebanon, and Egypt, where the Supreme Council of the National Evangelical Community in Syria and Lebanon and the Protestant Community of Egypt still hold some of their former functions. Religious groups in Israel also control personal law, although an overlapping system of civil courts does exist.

The church profiles that follow are divided into church families in the pattern of the Middle East Council of Churches. The particular churches or "denominations" are presented as they are listed by the MECC and the World Council of Churches. They are not equivalent to one another. For example, the Orthodox Church considers itself an international federation of churches, united in the same faith and order; there are national and regional bodies, but they are not separate denominations in the Protestant manner of speaking. The various Oriental Orthodox churches are fully independent from one another but they also are in full communion with each other.

The Catholic family includes the Latin Catholics, known as the Roman Catholic Church in the West, and Eastern Catholic churches that come under the Vatican's Congregation for the Oriental Churches. Although the synod of bishops of each particular church elects the heads of these churches, they must each gain approval of the Pope and are subject to the rules and regulations of the Holy See. The Evangelical church family includes individual denominations, each of which is completely independent.

In addition to the four church families represented in the Middle East Council of Churches, there are many small Protestant churches, a result of twentieth-century missionary movements, and a growing group of churches known variously as Hebrew Christians, Jewish Believers, or Messianic Jews. The latter see themselves in continuity with the earliest Judeo-Christian believers. These unaffiliated churches are listed as a separate category under the Evangelical church family.

Several conventions are used in reporting on specific church leadership: "b." means year of birth; "e." means year elevated or elected; "c." means year consecrated; "i." means year installed. The + sign before a telephone or fax number means that the international access code must be dialed according to the caller's particular country. In the United States and Canada the access code is "011."

The Eastern Orthodox Family

Introduction to the Eastern Orthodox Family

The Orthodox Church is defined as "an international federation of patriarchal, autocephalous [self-headed], and autonomous churches," according to the website of the Greek Orthodox Archdioceses in the United States. These autonomous churches are in communion with one another and deeply rooted in the same tradition; they are part of one church. The Orthodox churches do not recognize any council as ecumenical beyond the seventh council in 787 (Nicea II), but they revere those first seven councils as second only to the Bible in authority. Each of the churches, including the four traditional patriarchates, elects its own leadership (sometimes called a patriarch, metropolitan, or archbishop).

The term "Greek Orthodox," although often used, is misleading since it implies that the churches are part of the church of Greece or that they still use only Greek in their liturgy. It is an Orthodox custom to include in worship the language of the people who attend. Unfortunately, the use of the word "Greek" has implied to some political groups a close relationship with the country of Greece, sometimes causing persecution of the Orthodox. The term "Eastern Orthodox" is used here.

The system of patriarchates comes from the first few centuries of Christianity when all Christians in a given geographical area were considered to belong to the same church. At first each local church, headed by a bishop, was completely independent and not administratively subordinate to another bishop. By the third century a system developed wherein a number of dioceses would report to the bishop of the state capital. Later larger church administrative centers were formed, often corresponding to the administrative organization of the Roman Empire. The territorial principle is still the norm of organization although emigration has resulted in subordinate groups in other countries.

The Eastern Orthodox (or Byzantine Orthodox) churches are different in several ways from the Oriental Orthodox, who also have a patriarchal geographical system and who also use ancient liturgies. The Eastern Orthodox recognize the patriarch of Constantinople as Ecumenical Patriarch and "first among equals." They are sometimes called the Chalcedonian Orthodox, referring to their acceptance of the formula concerning the dual nature of Jesus Christ promulgated at the Council of Chalcedon in 451. Today the theological differences between the Eastern and Oriental Orthodox are considered matters of terminology, political pressures, and the slow pace of communication in the fifth century. Meetings of the two Orthodox branches have been held from time to time, led by the Ecumenical Patriarch and the Coptic Orthodox Pope.

The Middle East is not the area of the world with the most Eastern Orthodox members; that distinction belongs to Eastern Europe. Russia has the largest number of members with Romania in second place. Prince Vladimir of Kiev was baptized in Russia in 988 and, consistent with the customs of the time, the whole country became Eastern Orthodox. Moscow became known as the Third Rome (after Rome and Constantinople) and led in the conversion of neighboring areas. It was the Eastern Orthodox of the Middle East who suffered the most from the coming of Islam in the seventh century. Muslims considered the theology of the Trinity to be tritheism and the use of icons to be idolatry. Many Christians converted to Islam for socioeconomic as well as theological reasons.

The Orthodox, especially the Patriarchate of Constantinople, and the Roman Catholics grew apart during the first millennium because of a variety of factors; the date usually cited for the actual break is 1054. Two main issues were at stake: first, the idea of the universal supremacy and authority of the jurisdiction of the bishop of Rome and, second, the Roman Catholic changes to the Nicene Creed. The schism was finalized in the excommunications of 1054, but the Patriarchates of Antioch and Alexandria never made a formal break with Rome. Today the Eastern (Orthodox) and Western (Catholic) churches see themselves as "sister churches." A decisive event toward the re-establishment of communion was the meeting of Pope Paul VI and Patriarch Athenagoras of Constantinople in 1964 where they repealed the mutual anathemas of 1054.

Ecumenical Patriarchate of Constantinople

This great ancient center of the Christian church was founded around A.D. 36 by St. Andrew as the "Church of Byzantium." It came to great prominence when the city of Byzantium was made the capital of the Eastern Roman Empire in 331 by Constantine the Great and became known as the "New Rome" or Constantinople.

The Second Ecumenical Council in 381 recognized the See of Constantinople as a patriarchate and the Fourth Ecumenical Council in 451 recognized it as the first See of the East, second only to Rome. From the year 520 onward the Patriarch of Constantinople was recognized as the Ecumenical Patriarch, and after the schism of 1054 from the Roman Catholic Church the patriarchate emerged as the world center of the Eastern Orthodox Church. The patriarch has a special honor as "first among equals" *(primus inter pares),* with the right of convening pan-Orthodox conferences after consultation with primates of other Eastern Orthodox churches. He has limited authority and coordinates relations between the churches of the Orthodox communion.

During the Ottoman rule the Patriarch of Constantinople was regarded as the civil head of the entire Orthodox *millet* (p. 54) as well as the spiritual leader. He was free to govern all Orthodox in religious practices, commercial transactions, trade, marriage, and so on. The Ottomans also made the other patriarchs within the empire subordinate to Constantinople, in violation of the Orthodox principle of self-governing churches. In modern secular Turkey, which expresses considerable enmity toward Greece, the position of the Patriarch of Constantinople is precarious. To the Turks, the patriarch is the symbol of Greece and everything Greek, and 75 percent of the Greek Orthodox churches in Istanbul and its environs have been destroyed or badly damaged by Turkish mobs.

The Ecumenical Patriarchate was among the first to participate in the formation and development of the modern ecumenical movement. It still maintains its lead in ecumenism by promoting contacts with non-Eastern Orthodox churches, including the Oriental Orthodox, the Roman Catholics, the Anglicans, the Lutheran World Federation, the Reformed churches, and Islam and Judaism.

Despite urgings to move the patriarchate out of Turkey, the patriarch feels that residence in Istanbul, an international city at the crossroads of Europe and Asia, makes an ecumenical witness. He continues to have ultimate ecclesiastic authority over the monastic state of Mt. Athos in Greece, the exarchate of Patmos, the Church of Crete, and the Greek Orthodox in diaspora, including the Greek Orthodox Archdiocese of North and South America.

In Turkey itself, the patriarchate functions under a considerable number of restrictions. Since Turkish law limits higher education to government-controlled institutions, the historic seminary has been closed. The church still maintains elementary and high schools, monasteries and holy shrines, and various philanthropic and social associations and clubs. It also supports the Balouki Hospital, a mental hospital, an orphanage, a summer shelter for working girls, and a children's home. In diaspora, where most of the membership lives, there is a broad range of ministries.

Churches in the Patriarchate of Constantinople use the ancient Byzantine rite in the Greek language.

LEADERSHIP

His All Holiness Bartholomew I, Archbishop of Constantinople, New Rome, and Ecumenical Patriarch (b. 1940, e. 1991)

CONTACT INFORMATION

Address: Rum Patrikhanesi, 34220 Fener-Halic, Istanbul, Turkey
Tel.: +90.212.531.9670-6
Fax: +90.212.534-9037
E-mail: patriarchate@ec-patr.org
Website: www.patriarchate.org

MEMBERSHIP

The Greek Orthodox in the diaspora are part of the Ecumenical Patriarchate and number about 3,000,000, including some 8,000 in Turkey.

His All Holiness Ecumenical Patriarch Bartholomew

His full title may be Archbishop of Constantinople, New Rome, and Ecumenical Patriarch, but Patriarch Bartholomew has become known as the "Green Patriarch" because he has led in religious concern for the environment. During a 1987 symposium in California he emphasized the theological nature of environmentalism in these words: "How we treat the earth and all of creation defines the relationship that each of us has with God. It is also a barometer of how we view one another."

His All Holiness is the 270th successor to the Apostle Andrew and as Ecumenical Patriarch is the "first among equals" in the Eastern Orthodox communities. At the seventh general assembly of the World Council of Churches, Patriarch Bartholomew headed the Orthodox delegation and took a lead in expressing Orthodox objections to certain paths the WCC was pursuing. This has not deterred his ecumenical journey, however. He has continued to take leadership in the World Council of Churches and for eight years has been vice president of the WCC Faith and Order Commission.

He is quoted on his website as saying, "there has never been a greater need for spiritual leaders to engage themselves in the affairs of the world." To that end he has traveled widely, meeting with leaders of Orthodox and non-Orthodox churches, including Pope John Paul II, and with many heads of state.

Greek Orthodox Patriarchate of Jerusalem

The Greek Orthodox Patriarchate of Jerusalem is considered the oldest apostolic church and is often called "the mother of all churches." During the early centuries it was a bishopric under the metropolitan of Caesarea, but in 451 it became a patriarchate with special responsibility for protecting the holy places. After Constantine accepted Christianity as the state religion in the fourth century, magnificent churches were erected all over the area, especially at sites connected with Jesus. At about the same time monasticism came to Palestine from Egypt and flourished in the area between Jerusalem and the Dead Sea (the Judean desert).

The Holy Land was invaded numerous times by groups hostile to the Orthodox Church: by the Persians in 614, by the Muslims in 637, by the Latin crusaders in 1099, and by the Turks in 1517. In 638, when Caliph Omar ben Al-Khattab entered Jerusalem peacefully, he pledged to recognize the rights and privileges of the Orthodox Patriarch in Jerusalem. "Omar's Pledge," as it was called, also granted full freedom to the church in managing its religious and material affairs. The patriarch was recognized as the spiritual leader of the Christians. Neverthless, many Christians converted to Islam.

In 1099, the crusaders entered Jerusalem, installed a Latin Patriarch, and expelled the Greek Orthodox Patriarch. The Greek Orthodox Patriarchate functioned in Cyprus until 1177, when it returned to the Holy Land. Since then there have been numerous arguments over the protection of the holy places between the two patriarchates. A community of monks, known as the Brotherhood of the Holy Sepulchre, active since the fourth century, is charged by the Orthodox Patriarchate with defending the holy sites. The Brotherhood has conducted religious ceremonies at the Church of the Holy Sepulchre without interruption since 1177. The Status Quo (an 1852 declaration of the Ottoman Empire) set the parameters for all churches in many of the holy places, including times of liturgy, space to be occupied, and responsibility for upkeep and renovation. This arrangement has continued to the present.

The Orthodox patriarchs of Jerusalem have been of Greek origin and education. Members of the Brotherhood are Greeks and Arabs. The parish clergy are of Arab origin and serve the needs of the faithful. Within the Greek Orthodox communion the Jerusalem Patriarchate is ranked fourth after Constantinople, Alexandria, and Antioch. Because of the Jerusalem church's history and relative size, the Greek Orthodox Patriarchate is acknowledged by all churches in the Holy Land as first in ecclesiastical dignity in the Holy Land. In recent years this patriarchate has taken a conservative stand toward the ecumenical movement. When His Beatitude Diodoros I died the Israeli government tried to influence the choice of a new patriarch, and even after the election of His Beatitude Irineos I the Israeli government refused to recognize him. A new patriarch has been elected. The patriarch and his representatives interact with other church leaders, especially around issues concerning the status of Jerusalem and the impact of the military occupation on the Christian population in the Holy Land.

The patriarchate itself is in the Old City of Jerusalem and has jurisdiction over parishes in Jordan, Israel, territories administered by the Palestinian Authority, the Emirates, Qatar, and other small states. The church follows the Byzantine-rite liturgy of St. John Chrysostom, although in the local churches the liturgy is celebrated in Arabic. Because the hierarchy is Greek, the liturgy in monasteries and in the patriarchate is in Greek.

The patriarchate runs thirty-seven elementary and secondary schools as well as clinics and a housing project. The housing project is designed to help new young families stay in the Palestinian areas and Israel rather than emigrate to the West and was threatened as illegal in 2002 by the Israeli government. Parish priests are educated in a seminary of the patriarchate in Jerusalem and the hierarchy in monasteries in other countries. All clergy are given opportunities for theological study locally and abroad.

LEADERSHIP
His Beatitude Patriarch Theofilos III, Patriarch of Jerusalem

CONTACT INFORMATION
Address: Greek Orthodox Patriarchate, Christian Quarter, Old City,
    P.O. Box 14518, Jerusalem 91145
Tel.: +972.2.628.1033, +972.2.627.4941
Fax: +972.2.628.2048
E-mail: secretariat@jerusalem-patriarchate.info
Website: www.jerusalem-patriarchate.info

MEMBERSHIP
The Greek Orthodox Church is the largest Christian church in the Holy Land and Jordan with about 250,000 faithful. Their land holdings and buildings are extensive throughout Israel, Palestine, and Jordan, including agricultural lands as well as churches and holy sites.

Engineer Samer Laham

"Samer is the unknown soldier who works with us," says Imam Salak Quftara, son of the Grand Mufti of Syria. "Samer" is Samer Laham, associate general secretary of the Middle East Council of Churches and director of ecumenical relations at the Orthodox Patriarchate of Antioch. This compliment from a prominent figure in the Muslim community reveals the warmth with which the Muslims of Damascus regard this "unknown soldier."

Samer Laham has worked with the MECC since 1987 and has represented the Patriarchate of Antioch at the World Council of Churches. He was educated in civil engineering at Damascus University and his profession is the restoration and internal design of old and new buildings. As ecumenical officer and a major contact between Muslims and Christians in Syria, he is carrying out his profession by restoring and building not only churches but relations between Christians and Muslims as well. In 2008-2010 he also led an effort to assist Iraqi refugees who had fled to Syria. This effort had the support of several U.S. denominations.

Greek Orthodox Church of Antioch and All the East

Antioch was the place where the disciples were first called "Christians" (Acts 11:26). It was the capital of the Roman province in the East, and early Christians in Antioch were very influential in the complete separation of Christianity from Judaism. At the same time, the See of Antioch was very active in the ecumenical councils and in the debates that led to numerous schisms in the church. As a consequence of the Third Ecumenical Council, the Nestorian Church arose in Antioch, emphasizing the divine as the sole nature of Christ. When the teaching was banned, the believers fled to Persia, where the doctrine was welcomed.

The Patriarchate of Antioch was also divided by the statement of the Chalcedonian Council of 451 concerning the dual nature of Christ, with violent confrontations between the two factions. The non-Chalcedonians became an independent church known as the Syriac

Jacobite Church (now called the Syriac Orthodox Church) and the Chalcedonians continued as the Orthodox Church of Antioch. A further schism occurred when the monks of Maroun Monastery fled from persecution to the mountains of Lebanon and eventually became the Maronite Catholic Church.

After the Islamic conquest, the Orthodox in Antioch experienced some difficulties with local Muslims who misunderstood the church's good relationship with Constantinople as a civic rather than religious relationship. As time went on, however, many Christians from Antioch distinguished themselves as thinkers and writers in the Muslim world.

One of the first things the crusaders did when they occupied Antioch in 1098 was to deport the Orthodox clergy and install Latin bishops. Years later, when the Mamluks destroyed Antioch, the patriarch moved his see to Damascus. The Ottomans later conquered Damascus in 1516.

One final schism reducing membership further occurred within the Patriarchate of Antioch when a strongly pro-Catholic patriarch was elected. He was deposed and excommunicated by Constantinople but recognized by Pope Benedict XIII of Rome as the Patriarch of Antioch for the Melkite Catholic Church. There is a dialogue and cooperation between the Orthodox Church of Antioch and the Syriac Orthodox Church, including the sharing of spaces.

An international youth movement was launched from this patriarchate in 1942. The patriarchate maintains seventeen small monasteries, twenty-five primary schools, twelve secondary schools, and a hospital. The University of Balamand near Tripoli, Lebanon, is also part of the patriarchate's ministry. In addition to regular university courses, it provides theological training for priests.

The language of liturgy and prayers is Arabic in the Middle East but English in the United States. Some parts of the liturgy are still spoken in Greek.

LEADERSHIP
His Beatitude Ignatios IV Hazim, Patriarch of Antioch and All the
East (b. 1920, e. 1979)

CONTACT INFORMATION
Address: Bab Touma, P.O. Box 9, Damascus, Syria

Tel.: +963.11.542.4400/01/02/03
Fax: +963.11.542.4404
E-mail: antiochp@scs-net.org

MEMBERSHIP

The Patriarchate of Antioch is a self-conscious part of the Arab world, although there has been extensive emigration to North America, South America, Europe, and Australia. Parishes of the Church of Antioch are located in Lebanon, Syria, Iraq, Kuwait, Iran, the Americas, Europe, and Australia. It is estimated that there are 1,100,000 Greek Orthodox in Syria.

Greek Orthodox Patriarchate of Alexandria and All Africa

The church of Alexandria was founded by the apostle Mark in A.D. 40, and as such is the oldest Christian church in Africa. Ancient Alexandria was known for its library and schools so it was natural for the Christians to continue this tradition. By the fourth century, the Church of Alexandria had spread throughout Egypt and Libya and the Alexandrian Catechetical School had become the main center for training Christian theologians from all over the East.

In 451, after the Council of Chalcedon, the Church of Alexandria split into two patriarchates: the Egyptian, also known as the Coptic Patriarchate, and the Byzantine, which today is called the Greek Orthodox Patriarchate of Alexandria and All Africa. Following the Arab conquest in 640, the Greeks of Egypt suffered persecution because of their links to the Byzantine Empire and the suspicion that they were loyal to the empire.

After the Ottoman occupation of Egypt in 1517, the Greek Orthodox patriarchs were forced to seek temporary refuge in Constantinople. In Egypt today there are both Arab-speaking churches serving mostly Christians from Syria and Lebanon and Greek-speaking churches serving Greeks who were born in Egypt and those who immigrated.

Until the twelfth century the ancient Alexandrian rite was used but it was replaced by the Byzantine liturgy. Liturgical languages include Greek, Arabic, and several African languages. In the 1930s indigenous

East African Christians joined the Orthodox Church and their churches are served by African clergy in Kenya, Uganda, and Tanzania. Local churches in the southern parts of Africa primarily serve Greek expatriates. One of the great institutions of the patriarchate is the Greek Orthodox Library in Alexandria with over thirty thousand books and manuscripts dating to the ninth century. The major theological center for the training of East African clergy, "Makarios III," is located in Nairobi, Kenya.

The church maintains schools, clinics, and orphanages for the poor (including Muslims). For their own members there are a variety of activities, including Sunday schools, clubs, and Boy Scouts.

Within the Greek Orthodox communion the Patriarchate of Alexandria is recognized as second in dignity, following the Ecumenical Patriarchate of Constantinople. The church has played a significant role in the ecumenical movement, both in the region and throughout the world. The current patriarch Petros VII, and his predecessor Parthenios III, have been leaders of the Middle East Council of Churches.

LEADERSHIP

His Holiness Theodoros II, Pope and Patriarch of Alexandria and All
Africa for the Greek Orthodox (e. 2004)

CONTACT INFORMATION

Address: P.O. Box 2006, Alexandria, Egypt
Tel.: +203.486.8595
Fax: +203.487.5684
E-mail: info@patriarchateofalexandria.com
Website: www.patriarchateofalexandria.com

MEMBERSHIP

Membership is estimated by the patriarchate at 1,000,000. The growth in the patriarchate is in East and Central Africa, principally brought about by new black bishops from East Africa. The numbers in these dioceses are well beyond those in Egypt itself.

Greek Orthodox Church of Cyprus

The Orthodox Church of Cyprus traces its origins to the first Christian century, when the Roman proconsul was converted by Paul and Barnabas. The church was autocephalous (self-headed) from its establishment and was recognized by the Council of Ephesus in 431.

The island fell to Richard the Lionhearted during the Crusades and soon a Latin hierarchy was established with the monasteries and bishops placed under the authority of a Latin Archbishop of Cyprus. When the Ottoman Turks conquered Cyprus in 1571, the Latin hierarchy was banished and the Orthodox resumed electing their own archbishops. The Ottomans made the Archbishop of Cyprus the temporal as well as religious head of this Greek-speaking "nation." In 1821 when the Greek revolution broke out, the Turks considered the church sympathetic to the Greek cause and executed the archbishop and the bishops along with priests and other prominent churchmen. The Patriarchate of Antioch sent a new hierarchy to the island but the church still suffered under Turkish domination and later under British rule. The headquarters is in Nicosia.

Since 1974, the northern part of the island, which is predominantly Sunni Muslim, has been under Turkish occupation. (Since the history of the church and the island are so closely interwoven, see the section on Cyprus, page 145, where additional details can be found.)

The church sponsors women's unions, associations of scholars, and welfare projects, as well as catechetical schools in every parish. It has also built a pediatric hospital and institute and runs a church press for books and periodicals. The Archbishop Makarios III Foundation in Nicosia houses a well-respected collection of icons, paintings, and antiquities.

LEADERSHIP
His Beatitude Archbishop Chrysostomos II (b. 1927, e. 1977)

CONTACT INFORMATION
Address: The Holy Bishopric, Nicosia, Cyprus
Tel.: +357.2.430.696
Fax: +357.2.432.470
E-mail: office@churchofcyprus.org.cy
Website: http://www.churchofcyprus.org.cy

MEMBERSHIP INFORMATION

About 98 percent of all Christians in Cyprus belong to the Church of Cyprus. Although the membership of the church is virtually limited to the boundaries of the island, the church is active in encouraging the indigenous Orthodox in East Africa. The Church of Cyprus has built a seminary and a vocational school in Nairobi, even though the African churches are administratively part of the Patriarchate of Alexandria.

The Oriental Orthodox Family

An Introduction to the Oriental Orthodox Family

Although there are great differences among the Oriental Orthodox churches, early in their histories they all struggled to uphold their national interests against the imperial presence of the Byzantine and Persian Empires. The defining moment for each came in 451, when the Council of Chalcedon stated that Christ is one person in two natures "of one substance with the Father according to His divinity, of one substance with us according to his Humanity . . . in two natures without confusion, without change, without division, without separation." Those who rejected this formula believed that to say this was to over-emphasize the duality of Christ, and to compromise the unity of his person. Although the break in communion with the Eastern Orthodox still persists, there is official dialogue (p. 81). These churches are sometimes known as the non-Chalcedonian churches to distinguish them from those who accepted the doctrine.

In the case of the ancient Patriarchate of Alexandria, the vast majority of Egyptian Christians rejected the position of the Council of Chalcedon and, therefore, dominated the Patriarchate. They became the Coptic Orthodox Church. The minority, who accepted the Council, are today the Greek Orthodox Patriarchate of Alexandria. The situation was further complicated in Egypt by strong opposition at that time to Byzantine political and religious influences.

The Armenians were enmeshed in war and did not attend the Council in 451. Fifty-five years later they formally rejected the phrasing of Chalcedon and continued using Cyril of Alexandria's formula, "One is the nature of the Word Incarnate."

The "Western Syrians" (today's Syriac Orthodox Church) rejected Chalcedon on the ground that too many concessions had been made to the Nestorians (a group holding to the separation of the two natures of Christ). The Syriacs experienced considerable pressure from the Byzantine Empire and a split was provoked in the Antiochian community. The Syriac Orthodox Church was weakened by persecution from the Byzantines until the sixth century, when Yacub (Jacob) al-Baradai became Metropolitan of Edessa. He traveled widely and brought a revival to the church.

The heads of the Coptic, Syriac, and Armenian churches in the Middle East have been meeting annually to reaffirm their unity. (See the 1998 Common Declaration at the end of this chapter.) They do recognize each other's baptisms and are discussing statements of agreement on Christology as well as progress on meetings with other churches. The Oriental Orthodox churches are in communion with one another.

Armenian Apostolic Church
(Armenian Orthodox Church)

The origin of the Armenian Church dates back to the Apostolic Age. Christianity was preached in Armenia as early as the second half of the first century by two disciples of Jesus, St. Thaddeus and St. Bartholomew. During the first three centuries, Christianity in Armenia was a hidden religion under heavy persecution.

It was at the beginning of the fourth century (A.D. 301) that Christianity was officially accepted by the Armenian nation as the state religion. St. Gregory the Illuminator, the patron saint of the Armenian Church, and King Tiridates II, the ruler at the time, played pivotal roles in the Christianization of Armenia. Armenia thus became the first nation formally to adhere to Christianity. This conversion was followed in the fourth and fifth centuries by a process of institutionalization and Armenization of Christianity in Armenia.

The Armenian Apostolic Church, also referred to as the Armenian Orthodox Church, belongs to the Oriental Orthodox family of churches, together with the Coptic, Syriac, and Ethiopian churches. It accepts the first three ecumenical councils, and its theology and doctrine are based on the Apostolic faith — the teachings of the first three councils and of the early church fathers.

The head of the church is called the catholicos. The existence of two catholicoi and two catholicosates within the Armenian Church is due to historical circumstances. The Catholicosate of St. Etchmiadzin (the Catholicosate of All Armenians) is located in Etchmiadzin, Armenia. The Catholicosate of Cilicia is located in Antelias, Lebanon. In the tenth century, when Armenia was devastated by the Seljuks, many Armenians left their homeland and settled in Cilicia, where they reorganized their political, ecclesiastical, and cultural life. The catholicosate, the center of the church, also took refuge with the Armenians in Cilicia. It was first established in Hromkla but in 1293 was transferred to Sis, the capital city of the Armenian Kingdom of Cilicia. For nearly five centuries (the tenth through the fifteenth) the center of the Armenian political and ecclesiastical life was in Cilicia.

In the fifteenth century, Cilicia became a battleground between the Seljuks, Mamlukes, and other invading powers. In the meantime, there was relative peace in Armenia. The deteriorating situation in Cilicia, on the one hand, and a growing cultural and ecclesiastical awakening in Armenia, on the other, led the bishops and church leaders of Armenia to elect a catholicos (Kirakos Virapetsi) in St. Etchmiadzin. At that time, Krikor Moussabekiantz was the catholicos in Cilicia (1439-1446). Since 1441, therefore, there have been two catholicosates in the Armenian Church with equal rights and privileges within their respective jurisdictions. The Catholicosate of Cilicia always has recognized the primacy of honor of the Catholicosate of Etchmiadzin. The Armenian Apostolic Catholicosate of Cilicia is a part of the Middle East Council of Churches, but the Catholicosate of Etchmiadzin is not, since it is not located in the Middle East.

The liturgy of the Armenian Church was developed early in Christianity and continues to be celebrated in classical Armenian. The Eucharist and the preaching of the Word of God are at the center of the Armenian spiritual and liturgical life.

The Armenian Church Catholicosate of Cilicia

During the Armenian massacres (1915-1922) the Catholicosal See in Sis was confiscated and ruined by the Turks. The catholicos at the time, Sahad II, followed the traces of his flock. After a period of uncertainty, in 1930, the catholicosate was finally established in Antelias, Lebanon. Antelias is a small town situated four miles north of Beirut, the capital of Lebanon.

In the area of social diakonia, the Armenian Catholicosate of Cilicia administers an orphanage, a sanatorium, a housing project, and old people's homes in Lebanon, Syria, and Greece. Its publishing house produces hundreds of titles each year. The catholicosate has initiated a number of programs related to biblical studies, Sunday schools, popular lectures, and other activities through its department of Christian education. Youth and women's activities occupy an important place in the witness of the catholicosate.

LEADERSHIP
His Holiness Aram I Keshishian, Catholicos of Cilicia (b. 1947,
    o. 1968, e. 1995)

CONTACT INFORMATION
Address: Armenian Catholicosate of Cilicia, Antelias, Beirut, Lebanon
Tel.: +961.4.410.001/3
Fax: +961.4.419.724
E-mail: info@armenianorthodoxchurch.org
Website: www.armenianorthodoxchurch.org

MEMBERSHIP
This strong community, estimated at more than 200,000 members, has been thoroughly integrated into the Lebanese society. The Catholicosate of Cilicia also has major concentrations of believers in Syria (estimated at more than 25,000), Kuwait (10,000), the Gulf (10,000), Cyprus (8,000), Greece (30,000), Iran (300,000), North America (1,000,000 in the United States and 80,000 in Canada), and Venezuela (5,000).

H. H. Catholicos Aram I

"Unity points to what the church is to be and mission to what the church has to do." So says His Holiness Aram I, the Catholicos of Cilicia of the Armenian Apostolic Orthodox Church, in his best known book, a collection of essays entitled *The Challenge to Be a Church in a Changing World*. Then in his mid-fifties, Aram I was the youngest person ever to be elected as Moderator of the Central and Executive Committees of the World Council of Churches. He was born in Beirut, educated in Lebanon, Switzerland, England, and the United States, and has written more than a dozen books.

If in danger of thinking of His Holiness as simply an esoteric theologian, one has only to read carefully the content of his books and speeches. His commitment to ecumenism is equal to his commitment to solidarity with the oppressed and his concern for the integrity of creation. Catholicos Aram continues to define unity and mission by saying, "any attempt to separate unity and mission from social justice would be a denial of the true nature of the church."

(Quotations taken from *The Challenge to Be a Church in a Changing World* [New York: The Armenian Apostolic Church of America, 1997], p. 57 and p. 61.)

The Armenian Catholicosate of Etchmiadzin

Because the Catholicosate of Etchmiadzin is located in the Republic of Armenia neither it nor the judicatories related to it belong to the Middle East Council of Churches. Visitors and other Christians in the region, however, are aware that two Armenian patriarchates are located within the area. These are the Patriarchates of Jerusalem and Constantinople, and they do not belong to the MECC.

LEADERSHIP

His Holiness Karekin II, Catholicos of Etchmiadzin (b. 1951, e. 1999)

CONTACT INFORMATION
Address: Etchmiadzin, Republic of Armenia
Tel.: +374.31.53434, +374.1.151.198
Fax: +374.1.151.077

The Armenian Patriarchate of Constantinople

Autonomous in spiritual matters, the Patriarchate of Constantinople relates to the Catholicosate of Etchmiadzin. The patriarchate was begun in 1416 and was recognized by the Ottoman authorities as the sole legal representative of all Armenians in the empire.

This patriarchate operates at present under the strict religious laws of secular Turkey and, therefore, cannot sponsor institutions of higher education. Most of the congregations sponsor primary day schools. Current ministries include a large hospital, twenty church choirs, five associations, thirteen cultural associations, two sports clubs, four parish church schools, and an auditorium to provide continuing education and training in classical Armenian. The patriarchate publishes an *Academic Review,* an Armenian newspaper, and five monthly periodicals.

LEADERSHIP
His Beatitude Mesrob II, Patriarch of Constantinople (b. 1956,
e. 1998)

CONTACT INFORMATION
Tel.: +212.517.0970/1
Fax: +212.516.4833
E-mail: divan@armenianpatriarchate.org.tr

MEMBERSHIP
The patriarchate, located in Istanbul, includes churches in scattered locations in Turkey. The present Armenian population in Turkey (mostly in Istanbul) numbers 60,000. This is greatly reduced from the beginning of the twentieth century, before the massacre, when there were more than 2,000,000 Armenians living in what is now Turkey.

The Armenian Patriarchate of Jerusalem

The Armenian community in Jerusalem is perhaps the oldest outside Armenia. A resident community was established as early as the fifth century when pilgrims coming to the Holy Land decided to remain in the Holy City. (The first pilgrimages had taken place several centuries earlier.) The early functions of the Armenian Church in Jerusalem were to provide facilities for pilgrims and to safeguard the holy places. By 634 there were seventy Armenian churches in Palestine, mostly in Jerusalem. Both active monasteries and individual Armenian monks were central to the development of monastic life in the Judean desert. The Armenian Patriarchate of Jerusalem was established in 637 and since then has played a significant role in the development of the Jerusalem Christian community. In 1920, after the Armenian genocide, more than twenty thousand refugees arrived in Palestine. St. James Monastery is one of the oldest functioning monasteries in the Holy Land. The enclosed area of the Armenian Quarter in the Old City of Jerusalem houses most of the local Armenians along with pilgrims and provides an Armenian school and a museum open to the public.

LEADERSHIP

His Beatitude Torkom Manoogian, Patriarch of Jerusalem (b. 1919, e. 1990)

CONTACT INFORMATION

Address: Armenian Patriarchate, Armenian Patriarchate Road, Armenian Quarter, P.O. Box 14235, Old City, Jerusalem 91141 Israel
Tel.: +972.2.628.2331/628.4549
Fax: +972.2.626.4861/2
E-mail: arminf@netvision.net.il
Website: www.armenian-patriarchate.org

MEMBERSHIP

The Armenian population in Israel and the Palestinian Territories has gradually increased during the most recent two decades. This increase reverses a trend that began when the State of Israel was founded. Archbishop Aris Shirvanian, the church's director of ecumenical and foreign relations, credits the change to a new wave of Armenians from the former Soviet Union. By 2009 there were an estimated 2,000 in Jerusalem and environs, and an additional 18,000 in Tel Aviv, Jaffa, Petakh Tikva, Ashdod, Haifa, and Nazareth.

Coptic Orthodox Church

Egypt was a familiar place throughout the Old Testament and the place to which Jesus was taken by his family when they fled Herod's wrath. But tradition attributes the founding of the church in Egypt to the preaching and teaching of St. Mark, who is considered the first patriarch. Alexandria had been known for its library and schools long before the arrival of Christianity so it was natural for it to become the center of Christian learning. Many prominent bishops from the ancient world were instructed in the Alexandrian Catechetical School and played leading roles in the early councils. Alexandria also was the locus of severe persecutions by the Romans. As a result, the Coptic calendar begins with "the year of the martyrs," the year 284 in the common Western calendar.

Christian monasticism was born in the deserts of Egypt in an atmosphere that favored asceticism as a way to reach for heavenly life while still living in a physical body on earth. Its high point was the fourth century, when thousands of cells and caves housed hermits and monastic communities were formed both for women and for men. St. Anthony is considered the father of monasticism with his rule consisting of prayer and manual work. Although some were fully hermits for years, most of the monks followed the *coenobitic* system in which they lived alone in cells but came to the monastery for Saturday evenings and Sunday morning mass. They returned to their cells with food and materials to work with during the week. The monastic tradition has influenced the whole of the Coptic Orthodox Church, with its great emphasis on fasting (210 days a year) and spiritual retreats.

The Council of Chalcedon in 451 proved to be one of the most decisive moments in the history of the church in Egypt, reflecting both theological and political controversy. The Egyptian church had always maintained that state and religion should be separated, and it therefore resisted pressure from the Byzantine emperor to fall in line with

76

H. H. Pope Shenouda III

Consecrated in 1971, Pope Shenouda III's official title is "Pope of Alexandria and Patriarch of the See of St. Mark." He is an archeologist, a poet, and a prolific writer (of more than eighty books) who speaks seven languages fluently, and he has launched a revival in the Coptic Orthodox Church. In 1991 he was elected as one of the presidents of the World Council of Churches and in 1994 he was elected as a president of the Middle East Council of Churches, representing the Oriental Orthodox family of churches. His favorite role is still as teacher of the faithful, especially youth and young adults.

Pope Shenouda III has worked hard to nurture a constructive relationship with the Muslim community in Egypt and to encourage Christian unity throughout the world. He is in consultation with the Roman Catholic Church and signed a common declaration with Pope Paul VI in 1973 that expressed their mutual concern about church unity. He has been a leader in conversations among the several Oriental Orthodox churches and in the discussions with the Eastern Orthodox churches — there are few things that would give him more pleasure than overcoming the divisions dating from the Council of Chalcedon in 451.

Pope Shenouda III is proud of being an ecumenist and delights in positive movements toward a more united Christianity. He also knows that Christian "success" is often ephemeral and that persecution may once again be the fate of Eastern Christians. With a perpetual twinkle in his eyes, Pope Shenouda can talk about the problems of the church as well as the progress it has enjoyed. He reminds us that all but one apostle was a martyr, that most first-century bishops were martyrs, and that down through the ages there were many periods of persecution. "We may carry a cross, but we are happy carrying a cross," he says.

Chalcedon. The Coptic Church has continued its loyalty as a national church in the face of numerous conquests, persecutions, changes of government, and laws limiting personal freedom. At the same time it has maintained its independence from government control.

There are three main liturgies in the Coptic Orthodox Church: the Liturgy according to St. Basil, the bishop of Caesarea; the Liturgy according to St. Gregory of Nazianzus, the bishop of Constantinople; and the Liturgy according to St. Cyril I, the twenty-fourth pope of the Coptic Church. The Coptic language continues to be the liturgical language of the church, but it often appears in service books with the Arabic in parallel columns. Arabic is used in most of the priests' prayers.

The Coptic laypeople are very active in the church as members of parish councils and benevolent societies that help meet the pastoral and social needs of the community. There is also a popularly elected Coptic Lay Council to act as a liaison between the church and the Egyptian government and a joint lay/clergy committee to oversee and monitor the management of the Coptic Church's endowments.

Youth work is a special emphasis, with a bishop assigned to develop youth activities. Many of the youth act as Sunday school teachers; in Cairo alone there are thousands such young men and women serving as teachers.

The church is well established in all provinces of Egypt and in the Northern Sudan; there are parishes in Kuwait, Jordan, Lebanon, Iraq, and the Holy Land, and a diaspora of 1.2 million in the United States, Canada, Australia, Brazil, and several countries of Europe.

LEADERSHIP

His Holiness Pope Shenouda III (b. 1923, e. 1971), 117th Pope of Alexandria and Patriarch of the See of St. Mark

CONTACT INFORMATION

Address: Anba Rueis, 222 Ramses Street, Abbasiya, P.O. Box 9035, Cairo, Egypt

Tel.: +202.682.5357 and 5355

Fax: +202.2.282.5352 and 283.6691

Telex: OKINA UN 92333

E-mail: pope@copticpope.org

Website: www.copticpope.org

MEMBERSHIP

The Coptic Orthodox Church is the largest Christian community in the Middle East with about 6 million believers in forty-five dioceses.

Syriac (Syrian) Orthodox Church of Antioch and All the East

According to church tradition, St. Peter the Apostle founded the See of Antioch in 37. During the early centuries not only was Antioch the capital of Greater Syria but the patriarchate included the whole of Asia under its care. The patriarchate split as a result of the Council of Chalcedon in 451, when the Syriac Orthodox Church rejected the resolutions on the nature of Christ while the Greek Orthodox accepted them. There was continued Byzantine persecution of the Syriacs because of the rejection.

In the sixth century, St. Yacub (Jacob) al Baradai preached widely throughout the area, consolidating the faith and reviving the Syriac Orthodox Church. Members of the church are sometimes referred to as Jacobites to this day. The arrival of the Arab Muslims stopped the Byzantine persecution but led to Arab domination. The Mongol invasions in the late fourteenth century caused great difficulties, and churches and monasteries were destroyed and membership declined. At the end of the eighteenth century another decline occurred when the Syriac Catholic Church was formed as a result of Roman Catholic missionary activity. At the beginning of the twentieth century the church suffered persecution from the Turks, and after the collapse of the Ottoman Empire the Syriac Orthodox were massacred along with the Armenians.

Classical Syriac is still the liturgical language, and the form of the liturgy is attributed to St. James, brother of Jesus and the first bishop of Jerusalem. Syriac is considered a sacred language because Jesus, his mother, and the disciples spoke it; there are several Syriac expressions in the Bible even when it is translated into other languages. As the church expanded, several local languages (including Arabic, English, German, and Swedish) were also used in addition to Syriac. The use of the term "Syriac" instead of "Syrian" in the English name of the church is to emphasize the language of its origin rather than the location of its patriarch. It is considered a more accurate translation of the word "Suryani."

The Syriac Orthodox Church has a strong monastic tradition and a few monasteries survive in southeastern Turkey and other parts of the Middle East. A unique monastery of the diaspora is located in the Netherlands. New schools, new church buildings, and a home for the elderly have led to a renaissance for this church. In Sunday schools in the Middle East and the diaspora, Syriac is being taught in order to help preserve the ancient biblical language and the traditions and culture of this church. The administrative center of the church is in Damascus, Syria, with a concentration of members there and in Lebanon.

LEADERSHIP

His Holiness Moran Mor Ignatius Zakka I Iwas, Syriac Orthodox Patriarch of Antioch and All the East

CONTACT INFORMATION

Address: Bab Touma, P.O. Box 22260, Damascus, Syria
Tel.: +963.11.543.5918
Fax: +963.11.543.2400
E-mail: patriarch-z-iwas@scs-met.org
Website: http://sor.cua.edu

MEMBERSHIP

In addition to an estimated 250,000 members in the several Middle Eastern countries, notably in Syria and Lebanon, there are nearly 1,000,000 members in India. The church also has parishes in the Holy Land, Turkey, and India, and a significant diaspora in North America and Australia.

Meetings and Common Declaration
of the Oriental Orthodox

The patriarchs of the Coptic Orthodox Church, the Syriac Orthodox Church, and the Armenian Orthodox Church (Catholicosate of Cilicia) have agreed to a Common Declaration stating they want "to re-affirm our unity of faith and common ministry in the life of our people and all over the world, and explore together the most efficient ways and means to strengthen our common presence and witness in the [Middle East] region."

Some of their declarations include:

- affirming the common historical and doctrinal orientation of the three churches with an emphasis on the authority of the Council of Ephesus of 431;
- re-stating the churches' rejection of the classic Christian heresies of the past and their firm adherence to orthodoxy;
- asserting that "we will engage as a family of Oriental Orthodox Churches in the Middle East in any theological dialogue with other churches and Christian world communions";
- hoping for the inclusion of other churches of the Oriental Orthodox tradition in future meetings.[1]

During the last few years the Eastern Orthodox and Oriental Orthodox churches have been engaged in an official dialogue under the leadership of the Ecumenical Patriarch and the Coptic Orthodox Pope.

The patriarchs have been meeting regularly, appointing committees and reporting on progress in dialogues with the Anglican communion, the Roman Catholic Church, and the World Alliance of Reformed Churches.

1. A copy of the Common Declaration is available at http://sor.cua.edu/Ecumenism/200103170omtg4.html.

The Catholic Family

An Introduction to the Catholic Family

The Roman (or, as it is known in the East, the Latin) Catholic Church has had its own history in the West, but it is the relationship with the East that is important for understanding the Catholic church family in the Middle East. After the founding of Constantinople as the "New Rome" and the civic split between the Western and Eastern Roman Empires, the religious traditions grew apart with the development of separate liturgies and the use of different liturgical languages. Roman Catholic theology emphasized the Pope's (bishop of Rome's) worldwide jurisdiction while the Eastern churches believed that each patriarchal jurisdiction should be able to choose its own leader.

Although the Patriarchate of Rome and the various Greek Orthodox patriarchates agreed on the key issues at the Council of Chalcedon, there were numerous other events that eventually led to the schism. Certainly some of the non-Chalcedonian churches maintained contact with Rome, but the Oriental Orthodox family of churches worked more closely with the Eastern Orthodox than with the Western Catholics. When the Emperor of the West, Charlemagne, was crowned by the Pope of Rome in 800, it signaled an end to a single tradition of Empire.

By the ninth century, the controversies over how a creed could be modified also had become divisive, so that in 1054, when the mutual excommunication occurred between Rome and Constantinople, there was already a coolness to the relationship. The Crusades followed only fifty years later, originally with the encouragement of Constantinople.

The establishment of the Latin Patriarchate in Jerusalem, however, on property that had belonged to the Orthodox Patriarchate, and the sack of Constantinople during the Fourth Crusade, completely severed the relationship.

Several attempts were made to bridge the gap, but they failed. The gulf was widened when five different Eastern-rite Catholic churches were established as new patriarchates between 1552 and 1824. These are the Chaldean Catholics, the Greek Catholics or Melkites, the Armenian Catholics, the Syriac Catholics, and the Coptic Catholics. These churches are organically related to Rome but each retains the liturgy of its Orthodox heritage and its traditional language. Most Orthodox consider these churches to be an obstacle in the way of reconciliation with the Roman Catholic Church, although some of these churches see themselves as ecumenical bridges. The 1964 meeting between Patriarch Athenagoras of Constantinople and Pope Paul VI marked the beginning of this new rapprochement. Visits have continued and the question seems to be whether particular issues are "church-dividing differences" or merely a different theological approach exacerbated by centuries of separation. (See pp. 51-52 for some issues.) The Catholic family became a part of the Middle East Council of Churches in 1990, the only major council of which it is a part. The system of church families, rather than pure denominational membership, encouraged this possibility.

Although they retain the Eastern character of their life and worship, the Eastern-rite Catholic churches have adopted some traditions from the Roman Catholic Church. Syriac Catholics, for example, say the rosary.

All of the Catholic churches in the Middle East except the Latin Patriarchate are related to the Vatican through the Congregation for the Oriental Churches in the Roman Curia. They elect their own patriarchs, who must then be approved by the Pope. Although Vatican II stated the equality of the Eastern Catholic churches with the Latin Church, when they meet the Latin Patriarch chairs the meeting.

Armenian Catholic Church of Cilicia

This church has its origins among Armenian Christians who accepted the doctrines of the Council of Chalcedon in 451 and maintained communion with the churches of Constantinople and Rome. Armenians at that time lived in a vast Christian kingdom that stretched from the Caucasus to the Black Sea; there was a major concentration of Armenians in the region known as Cilicia in southern Turkey. The majority of these Armenians rejected Chalcedon and became the Armenian Apostolic Church, one of the Oriental Orthodox churches.

When the twelfth-century crusaders from Europe, especially France, made their way to the Holy Land through Cilicia they formed an alliance with the Armenian king, many of whose people had favored the West when the Catholic and Orthodox churches separated in 1054. Cilicia was known as "lesser Armenia," and the "unionist" wave remained strong there even though the king's action was unpopular with the majority who lived in "greater Armenia." The people of Cilicia also welcomed the Dominican, Franciscan, and Jesuit monks who arrived after 1439 to train clergy and laity and to cement relations with Rome.

That year, at the Council of Florence, a decree of reunion, *Exultate Deo,* was published affirming ties between Armenian Christians and Latin Christians. Although there were no immediate actions taken as a result, the decree formed the basis for the establishment of the Armenian Catholic Church.

During a period of political and religious turmoil, the Armenian Catholic bishops met in Aleppo (Syria) in 1740 and elected a patriarch-catholicos for the Catholic branch of the Armenian church. Pope Benedict XIV confirmed Bishop Abraham Ardzivian as Patriarch of Cilicia of the Armenians in 1742. The new patriarch took the name Abraham Pierre I; all successive Armenian Catholic bishops have included the name "Peter" (Pierre, Bedros, Petros, etc.) in their titles. His patriarchal see was installed in Lebanon in 1743 at the Convent of Kraym and was moved in 1749 to the Convent of Bzoummar. In 1867 the see was moved to Istanbul but later was returned to Lebanon; the see today is located in Beirut. The Ancient Armenian language is used for worship in the church, but services follow the general liturgical patterns of the Roman Catholic Church.

Like all Armenians, the Armenian Catholics suffered greatly in the genocide that preceded and followed World War I, and their community was decimated. Members of the Armenian Evangelical Church and of the Orthodox and Catholic communities enjoy generally cordial relations with one another today, and there is significant sociocultural collaboration and intermarriage among members of the three churches.

Pastoral and educational ministries were re-energized as a response to the Armenian genocide and include service to widows and orphans and an intentional ministry to Armenians who have emigrated to Europe, Australia, and North and South America. Youth clubs, scout groups, and women's clubs have been organized, as well as services to university students. Most of the programs are offered to all Armenians, whether Catholic, Orthodox, or Evangelical. With the collapse of the Soviet Union, ministries to Armenian Catholics have been developed in the Republic of Armenia in collaboration with the Armenian Apostolic Catholicos of Etchmiadzin.

LEADERSHIP
His Beatitude Nersis Bedros IX is the current catholicos and patriarch (e. 1999)

CONTACT INFORMATION
Address: Rue Hopital Orthodox, Jehtawi-Achrafieh, Beirut, Lebanon;
Tel.: +961.1.570.556
Fax: +961.1.570.563
E-mail: patrarca@magnarama.com

MEMBERSHIP INFORMATION
There are an estimated 550,000 Armenian Catholics worldwide. The largest numbers of Armenian Catholics live in and around Beirut, Lebanon, and Aleppo, Syria. Others reside elsewhere in Lebanon and Syria as well as in Iraq, Turkey, Egypt, and Iran, and in diaspora. There is a small community in Jerusalem and Amman, Jordan. Nearly 35,000 live in the United States and another 10,000 in Canada. They are part of a new diocese created in 2005 by Pope Benedict XVI.

Chaldean Catholic Church of Babylon

At the time of the Crusades, Dominican and Franciscan missionaries began work among the members of the Assyrian Church of the East. In 1289 the renowned Franciscan, John of Montecorvino, carried a letter from Pope Nicholas IV to Yabalaha III, the catholicos of the Church of the East. The catholicos was said to have been "well disposed toward the Catholic Church." Nevertheless, it was not until the mid–sixteenth century that the first Chaldean Catholic Church emerged.

When, in 1552, some bishops in the ancient Assyrian Church of the East rejected the hereditary succession of a minor (Simon VIII Denha) to the patriarchal throne, they elected Abbot Yuhannan Sulaka as patriarch and sent him to Rome to arrange a union with the Catholic Church. In April of 1553, Pope Julius III ordained him a bishop and proclaimed him Patriarch Simon VIII of the Chaldeans. The name Chaldean was used to suggest the traditional origin of the Magi who came from the East to celebrate Jesus' birth.

Returning to his homeland from Rome, the new Patriarch Simon began a series of reforms, but the Patriarch of the Assyrian Church arranged to have the Pasha of Amadya capture him. Simon was tortured and executed in 1555. A long period of conflict between the two churches followed, with the Chaldeans eventually becoming the larger church. Ecclesiastical stability finally was achieved between them after 1900, even though the Chaldeans suffered heavily from massacres during World War I. Despite the fact that nearly twenty thousand of the faithful were killed (in addition to three bishops and many priests) the membership of the church grew spectacularly until the mid-1940s.

The patriarchate was moved from Mosul to Baghdad in 1950, when many members of the church migrated from northern Iraq. The greatest concentration of members is in Baghdad, Iraq. Throughout that country there are nine dioceses, as well as three in Iran and five in other parts of the Middle East. Chaldean communities in the Middle East (listed in order of size) are also located in Turkey, Syria, Lebanon, Kuwait, Jordan, and Egypt.

The Chaldean (East Syriac) liturgy is celebrated in the Eastern dialect of Syriac. It is an abbreviated form of the ancient liturgy of the holy apostles still used in the Assyrian Church of the East. Over the years, some Latinization of both format and phrasing has taken place and all Christological references are in keeping with Roman Catholic traditions.

The church has long had special interests in education and in pastoral care of its members. The Chaldean Sisters of Mary Immaculate are at work in eight centers in five nations serving in primary and secondary schools, kindergartens, and orphanages. The use of European personnel in several institutions was phased out during the last quarter of the twentieth century.

Following the 1991 Gulf War both Muslims and Christians have experienced widespread suffering. Water-borne diseases such as typhoid fever, polio, and hepatitis A reached epidemic proportions after water purification plants were bombed.

LEADERSHIP

Cardinal Mar Emmanual III Delly, Patriarch of Babylon of the Chaldeans (b. 1927, e. 2003)

CONTACT INFORMATION

Address: P.O. Box 6112, Baghdad, Iraq
Tel.: +964.1.887.9604
Fax: +964.1.884.9967
Website: http://www.st-adday.com

MEMBERSHIP

The church estimates its membership as nearly 750,000, mainly in Iraq, where it is by far the largest Christian group. In addition, there are about 180,000 Chaldeans who belong to twelve parishes in the Diocese of St. Thomas the Apostle of Detroit of the Chaldeans. Elsewhere in the diaspora, in Australia, Canada, France, England, Sweden, Greece, Italy, and the United States, the Chaldean Catholics are under the spiritual care of local Latin (Roman) Catholic bishops.

Coptic Catholic Church of Alexandria

One of the three modern churches that trace their beginnings to the Apostle Mark, the Coptic Catholic Church is drawn from both sides of the great schism of Chalcedon. Theologically, the early Egyptian Catholics defended the resolutions of the council. Their patriarchate was headed at times by a pro-Chalcedonian Orthodox and at other times by a (Chalcedonian) Catholic patriarch, until gradually the prominence of Greek Orthodox expatriates in Alexandria became dominant. In the confused period that followed, it became customary for Catholic priests to come at intervals from Jerusalem to offer the sacraments to those who desired to maintain ties to the Roman Catholic Church.

As an outgrowth of the Crusades, Franciscan missionaries were active in the Holy Land during the seventeenth century, and by the year 1741 a Coptic Orthodox (non-Chalcedonian) bishop stationed in Jerusalem declared himself a Catholic. Pope Benedict XIV then gave the Jerusalem bishop Athanasios responsibility for the scattered groups of Catholics in Egypt. Because of the sensitive political situation in Egypt, however, Athanasios was represented by a vicar.

Unable to build their own churches because of Ottoman rule, the Catholic Copts worshiped in Franciscan churches. By 1829, when the Ottoman authorities authorized them to build their own places of worship, the church was well developed and the Catholic Patriarchate of Alexandria was firmly established. In another reversal, a decade after Cyril Makarios was consecrated as Patriarch Cyril II of the Catholic Copts in 1899, he resigned to join the Greek Orthodox. The patriarchate then was served by apostolic administrators until 1947, when Msgr. Mark Khuzaam was elected patriarch.

The Coptic Catholic Church contributes energetically to the Arab renaissance in Egypt, especially through scholarly preparation and translation of theological books. Monasticism in this church is more diversified and less contemplative than that in the Coptic Orthodox Church. The Jesuit, Franciscan, and Lazarist orders have been active within the Coptic Catholic Church for several centuries, and the Egyptian Sisters of the Sacred Heart play a major role. The church places high priority on work with youth and women, convinced that it must actively help preserve Christian values and church traditions. The church also puts priority on helping its members live as effective citizens in a society that faces many internal and external pressures.

The liturgy is an abbreviated form of the service still used by the Coptic Orthodox, from which it was derived. Some priests sing the central part of the liturgy in the ancient Coptic language, although there is an increasing use of Arabic in all services.

LEADERSHIP
His Beatitude Stephanos II Ghattas, Patriarch of Alexandria of the
   Copts (b. 1920, e. 1986)

CONTACT INFORMATION
Address: 42 Ibn Sandar-Kobri Al Kubbah, P.O. Box 69, Saray Al
   Kubbah, Cairo 11712, Egypt
Tel.: +20.2.259.9494 or 257.1740
Fax: +20.2.454.5766
E-mail: jeannebuisson@yahoo.fr

MEMBERSHIP

In addition to an estimated 300,000 believers who live in six metropolitan dioceses along the Nile, there are at least 10,000 in the diaspora. Those who live in the diaspora — in Australia, Canada, France, and the United States — are under the care of local Catholic bishops. The six dioceses in Egypt are served by 175 local priests (some of whom are married, in the Eastern tradition) and by several monastic priests. The Coptic Catholic Church is the largest Catholic body in Egypt and the only one that is growing.

Greek Melkite Catholic Patriarchate of Antioch, Alexandria, and Jerusalem

The name "Melkite" is drawn from the Syriac and Arabic words for ruler or king, *melki* and *malik*. It was applied, disparagingly, by the so-called Monophysites to those who supported the Council of Chalcedon. The word came to designate orthodoxy and was used for centuries to refer to the sees of Alexandria, Antioch, and Jerusalem. Today it refers to the Byzantine (Orthodox) Catholics who were drawn from those three patriarchates.

These three patriarchates did not participate in the historic mutual excommunications of 1054 between the churches of Rome and Constantinople. They continued to share liturgical ties with Constantinople, but maintained contact with Rome. During the sixteenth and seventeenth centuries, the presence of Latin-rite missionaries stimulated relationships between Antioch and Rome. Internal tensions and resistance from Constantinople, however, prevented the establishment of full communion, despite general support in Antioch.

In 1724, upon the death of Patriarch Athanasios III Debbas, rivalry between the two groups, centered in Damascus and Aleppo, Syria, came to a head. Both groups elected successors to Athanasios. The Damascus party named a strongly pro-Catholic man who took the name Cyril VI. With the approval of the Patriarch of Constantinople, the Aleppo group named Sylvester. The Ottoman government (also located in Constantinople) recognized Sylvester, and Cyril was forced to seek refuge in Lebanon. Five years later, Cyril's election was recognized by Pope Benedict XIII. Full communion between Cyril's followers and Rome was established in 1744.

H. B. Gregorius III Laham

The patriarch of the Greek Catholic (Melkite) Church is well known in terms of his former position as His Eminence Archbishop Lutfi Laham, the Patriarchal Vicar General in Jerusalem. Born in Dariya, Syria, and brought up as a monk, His Beatitude earned a Ph.D. from the Oriental Institute in Rome and has written several books on spiritual life. He was chosen patriarch in 2001. At his investiture he spoke of himself as, first of all, a servant, and only then a patriarch, which means the titles have the same meaning. He also stressed his commitment to ecumenism and the Melkite Church's close relationship with the other churches of Antioch.

In Jerusalem, the then archbishop was known for his ecumenical spirit, his ready smile, and his welcome to visiting Christians. He established a museum at the church to teach about various churches in the Holy Land (not just the Melkite Church) and provided translations of the liturgy to those in attendance at services. He speaks Arabic, French, German, Italian, Latin, Greek, and English and was known to extend greetings and preach parts of his sermon in those languages to visitors at the services. He was also a leader in ecumenical relations between the heads of churches and championed the cause of the local indigenous Christians.

Following a time of government hostility and persecution, the Ottomans formally recognized the Melkite Catholic Church. A period of growth followed, partly because the Melkites were perceived as being pro-Arab while the Orthodox Patriarchate of Antioch was seen as being tied politically to Ottoman Constantinople. Because of the changed demography, in 1838 the cities of Alexandria and Jerusalem were added to Antioch in the formal title of the Melkite Patriarch.

Melkites have celebrated the Byzantine rite for more than one thousand years, drawing on the norms and liturgical customs of Constantinople from the end of the eighth century. Although they have been in communion with Rome since the time of the Crusades, the church resisted Latinization. Baptism is by immersion and leavened bread is used in Communion. The faithful cross themselves from right to left in the manner of the Eastern churches.

During the Second Vatican Council, Maximos IV Sayegh argued forcefully against the Latinization of the Eastern Catholic churches, urging Roman Catholics to be more receptive to the authentic, ancient, Oriental Christian traditions. Many Melkite cathedrals and parish churches contain outstanding examples of Byzantine icons and frescoes.

Today Greek Catholics look back to the time before 1054, when the great rupture took place between Rome and Constantinople, between West and East, and they look forward to the time when that breach will be healed. By their own testimony, the Melkites are "very active in fostering reconciliation between East and West." They are uniquely positioned to do just that, especially within the Catholic family of churches. Because many of the leaders of this church have traveled and studied in Europe and the Americas, they have also reached out to Evangelicals (Protestants), offering a friendly window to the Byzantine religious traditions. Melkite bishops generally favor the reunification of their church with the Orthodox Patriarchate of Antioch when reconciliation is achieved.

Especially in areas of human need, the church provides social and educational services. Among its own laity the church offers both a teaching and a pastoral ministry. With its accent on a sung liturgy, the church provides opportunities for choirs through which the members learn much theology. The church also seeks to foster Christian-Muslim dialogue.

LEADERSHIP

His Beatitude Gregorius III Laham, Patriarch of the Greek Catholic Church, Patriarch of Antioch and All the East, of Alexandria, and of Jerusalem (b. 1933, e. 2001)

CONTACT INFORMATION

Address: The principal see is at Bab Sharki, Haret Al Zaitoun, P.O. Box 22249, Damascus, Syria

Tel.: +963.11.544.6529 and 541.4531

Fax: +963.11.541.8966

The Patriarch is also entitled to live in the various centers of the church and has another major office at Raboueh, P.O. Box 70071, Antelias, Lebanon

Tel.: +961.4.525.655 or 961.4.525.301

Fax: +961.4.418.113
E-mail: gcp@pgc-lb.org
Website: www.pgc-lb.org

MEMBERSHIP

Recent estimates number the faithful at just over 1,000,000, of whom approximately half are living in the Middle East. Next to the Maronites, the Greek Catholic (Melkite) church is the largest Catholic community in the region. With membership concentrated in Lebanon, Syria, Jordan, Israel, and the occupied West Bank (including Jerusalem), the church also has a significant number of parishes in Egypt, and a few parishes in the north of the Sudan. In addition, Melkites live in Turkey and Iraq, as well as in a growing diaspora in North and South America.

Latin Patriarchate of Jerusalem

From before the time of Christ, imperial Rome was present in the Holy Land. The involvement of Roman officials was recorded in the Gospel narratives of Jesus' birth, ministry, and death, and the early church spread into southern Europe along Roman roads and sea-lanes. The church in Rome was the product of the work of the apostles Peter and Paul; in the West it is better known as the Roman Catholic Church.

As the church grew and specific territorial jurisdictions called patriarchates were defined, Rome — as the seat of the empire — was first in ecclesiastical precedence, followed by Alexandria and Antioch. Later Constantinople was designated a patriarchate and, in 451, Jerusalem. These patriarchates remained in communion with each other despite divisions within particular patriarchates and the debates among theological parties.

Numerous points of difference developed between the Patriarchate of Rome (which used Latin in the liturgy) and the Patriarchate of Constantinople (which used Greek). Along with language differences and the political developments that separated East from West, there were also divergent understandings of the nature of the church. The West unilaterally added "from the Son" (filioque) to the description of the procession of the Holy Spirit in the Nicene Creed. In 1054 (which is often considered the breaking point between Eastern and Western

H. B. Patriarch Michel Sabbah
(former Latin patriarch of Jerusalem)

Patriarch Michel Sabbah was named by Pope John Paul II as the first Palestinian Arab Latin Patriarch of Jerusalem. As chairperson of the Synod of Catholic Bishops in the Middle East, Patriarch Sabbah played a leading role in bringing the Catholic family of churches into membership in the Middle East Council of Churches. He has also encouraged other church leaders in Jerusalem to meet regularly in response to Israeli occupation of the West Bank, including the Old City in East Jerusalem, and has been a leader in pursuing peace in the region.

Born in Nazareth, Patriarch Sabbah began his preparation for the Catholic priesthood at the age of ten. In addition to local parish work, he has served as president of Bethlehem University and earned a Ph.D. at the Sorbonne in Paris. His passion for ecumenism and his awareness of the forces dividing the religions in Jerusalem have led him to write and to help prepare many statements and pastoral letters on the subject. Patriarch Sabbah realizes that the Catholic Church and the Orthodox churches equally trace their lineage to Jerusalem and the Church of Pentecost, and in his own quiet way he is seeking to mend the ruptures that have divided the Body of Christ. "We cannot remain divided. We will, naturally, remain different. But we must be one people who serve the Lord Jesus together," says the Latin Patriarch. He longs for the time when there will be "[only] one patriarch in Jerusalem and another one, for example, in Antioch. It will take time but it is a goal toward which we all must walk."

churches) the papal legate of the Patriarchate of Rome and the Patriarch of Constantinople excommunicated each other. Although the other patriarchates were not parties to that rift, most of them gradually sided with Constantinople.

Less than fifty years later, in 1099, crusaders from Europe marched on Jerusalem and the wedge between Eastern and Western Christianity was driven deeper. Even before the crusaders entered the Holy City, the Greek Patriarch was forced to flee to Cyprus. The property of the local Greek Orthodox Patriarchate was confiscated by the civil authorities and then given to the Latin Church; this led to the establishment of a Latin (Catholic) Patriarchate.

Jerusalem fell into Muslim hands in 1187 and the Latin hierarchy escaped to Cyprus and then to Europe. Forty years later the Franciscans were allowed into the Holy Land by the Muslims. In 1342 Pope Clement VI formally declared the Franciscans "custodians" of the Holy Land and provided an official Latin presence through the "custos," who is also known as the "Guardian of Mt. Zion."

Eventually, in 1847, a Latin Patriarch returned to the Holy Land to function side by side with the Custos of the Holy Land. Claims to the holy places among the Latins, Greeks, and Armenians (aided and abetted by several European governments) caused flare-ups until, in 1852, the Ottoman government issued the *firman* (decree) known today as the "Status Quo," which defines the role of each of the churches in several holy sites.

The patriarchate provides spiritual and educational ministries to the clergy and faithful of the Holy Land while the Franciscans are considered custodians of the holy sites. Since the Vatican maintains a papal nuncio in Jerusalem and negotiates directly with the government of Israel, there are three focal points for Roman (Latin) Catholicism in the Holy Land — the patriarchate, the custos, and the Vatican representative. The latter has made agreements with both the Israeli government and the Palestinian Authority on behalf of the churches.

Especially under the previous patriarch, Michel Sabbah, the church has been an outspoken advocate for the religious and civil rights of Christians in Israel and the occupied West Bank, including East Jerusalem. The patriarchate also maintains ecclesiastical contact with dozens of Catholic religious orders and institutions, many of which are sponsored by foreign or international agencies.

The patriarchate itself sponsors schools and social service institutions that minister to Muslims as well as to Christians. In addition to "guarding" the holy places, the Franciscans also have encouraged the growth of local churches and social service institutions. Because of the unique nature of the Holy Land for all Christians, the patriarchate offers significant ecumenical leadership and reaches out to Jewish and Muslim officials as well.

Liturgical events in the parish churches follow the Latin rite and are conducted in Arabic. Because the patriarchate and its churches serve a broad international community of pilgrims, students, expatriates, and others, worship is also conducted in several other languages, including Latin.

LEADERSHIP

His Beatitude Msgr. Fouad Twal, Latin Patriarch of Jerusalem
  (b. 1940, e. 2008)

CONTACT INFORMATION

Address: Latin Patriarchate Road, Christian Quarter, P.O. Box 14152,
  Old City, Jerusalem 91141
Tel.: +972.2.628.2323
Fax: +972.2.627.1652
E-mail: chancellery@latinpat.org
Website: http://www.lpj.org

MEMBERSHIP

Parishes related to the patriarchate are located in Palestine, Israel, Jordan, and Cyprus. In addition to an estimated 70,000 Arab members of parish churches, there are several thousand resident expatriates who work and study. There are around 2,000 religious men and women from several congregations.

Maronite Church of Antioch and All the East

The Maronite Church is named for its founder, St. Maron, who as a priest lived a monastic life in the mountains of Syria near Antioch. Within fifty years of his death, around 410, Maron's followers developed a strong sense of identity and community life. They participated in the Council of Chalcedon (451) and fully adopted, and later actively propagated, Chalcedon's position on the two natures of Christ.

According to Maronite tradition and to the writings of the Syriac Orthodox Patriarch and historian Denys of Tell Mahre, the Maronite

Antiochian Patriarchate was established at the end of the seventh century, some fifty years after the Islamic conquest. Throughout their history the Maronites suffered greatly to retain their spiritual and temporal autonomy. Following the destruction of the great monastery of St. Maron on the Orontes River at the end of the tenth century, they moved their patriarchate to Mount Lebanon.

Relations between the Maronites of Mount Lebanon and the crusaders (1099-1291) were generally good and helped the continuation of Maronite ties with the Roman See. The Maronites, who have some practices from the Roman Catholic tradition, consider themselves never to have been separated from Rome. The fall of Tripoli in 1291, however, led to renewed persecutions at the hands of the Mamluks in the fourteenth and fifteenth centuries. In 1440 the patriarchal see was transferred from the area of the Mayfuq monastery near Batrun to the Qannubin monastery in the Qadisha Valley in North Lebanon.

The Council of Trent (1545-1563) and the establishment of the Maronite College in Rome in 1584 led to what qualifies as a "Maronite Renaissance," an intellectual golden age with several prominent Maronite scholars. That renewal, together with an expanding demography of Maronites into the most southerly parts of Mount Lebanon, led them to play an active role in the public life of their region.

After World War I, while their identity and freedom were still threatened, Patriarch Elias Howayyek attended the Paris Peace Conference in 1919. A somewhat autonomous Lebanon resulted, within internationally recognized natural frontiers, under a French mandate. In 1943, a National Covenant provided a delicate balance between Christians and Muslims in Lebanon. By agreement, the country's president would always be a Maronite, the speaker of the parliament a Shi'ite, and the prime minister a Sunni.

In 1975 the so-called Lebanese Civil War began, lasting until 1990. One of the consequences of this war was the 1989 Ta'if Agreement, which distributed parliamentary seats equally between Christian and Muslim communities. The agreement kept the presidency of the Lebanese Republic in the hands of a Maronite, although with somewhat diminished powers. Despite a new wave of emigration, it seems clear that the Maronites and their church will continue to be a force for an independent Lebanon in which citizens would enjoy maximum freedoms.

Inspired by the papal visit to Beirut in May 1997, and by the Post

Synodal Apostolic Exhortation, "New Hope for Lebanon," the Maronite Church works actively for human rights, the development of democratic institutions, the promotion of women's status in society, and the reconciliation of the Lebanese people through dialogue among the different religious families.

Several monastic orders and congregations (men and women) have contributed to the development of the Maronite Church spiritually, intellectually, and socially. Together with the patriarchal see, they operate schools and universities, hospitals, orphanages, and asylums, as well as new forms of communication (magazines, television, radio, fax, e-mail, and the use of the Internet).

The Maronite liturgy is rooted in the Syriac Antiochian tradition, but after the sixteenth century the liturgy was influenced by some Latin practices. Maronites pray in the various languages of their countries of residence.

LEADERSHIP

His Beatitude Mar Nasrallah Boutros Cardinal Sfeir (b. 1920, e. 1986)
is the Maronite Patriarch of Antioch and All the East

CONTACT INFORMATION

Address: Bkerke, Lebanon
Tel.: +961.9.915-441 or 936-488
Fax: +961.9.933-501
E-mail: sfeir@bkerke.org.lb
Website: www.bkerke.org.lb
E-mail of patriarchal secretary: SecGEN@BKERKE.ORG.LB

MEMBERSHIP

Maronites count between six and seven million adherents worldwide, about one million of whom live in Lebanon. The Maronites form the largest Christian community in Lebanon. The church also has parishes in Syria, Egypt, the Holy Land, and Cyprus, and there are major concentrations in North and South America and in Australia. Those who live overseas are much larger in number than those in Lebanon itself but they retain a strong religious identity and Lebanese loyalty.

Syriac (or Syrian) Catholic Church of Antioch

The Apostolic character of this church, along with the other Syriac and Antiochian churches, is drawn from the spread of early Christianity from Jerusalem to Antioch and Aramaic Syria. Following the Council of Chalcedon in 451, there was a split in the Antiochian church, with the Syriac Orthodox Church rejecting the council's teachings and the Byzantine Orthodox, along with the Patriarchate of Rome, endorsing the doctrines. The Syriac Catholic Church has its roots in the Syriac Orthodox Church (non-Chalcedonian). Currently the church uses "Syriac" instead of "Syrian" in English since it refers to the language of the church and its origin rather than to the present nation of Syria.

Some Syriacs maintained close ties to the Western (Latin) church, and during the Crusades numerous friendly relationships developed between Catholic and Syriac Orthodox bishops. The relative isolation of parish priests and their members, however, meant that they were less inclined toward the initiatives from Rome for an actual union. A decree of union enunciated during the Council of Florence in 1444 never materialized.

Educational efforts in Aleppo, one of the main Syriac Orthodox centers, by Jesuit and Capuchin missionaries in the early seventeenth century led a number of priests and many faithful to convert to Catholicism. By 1662, a leader of the Catholic party was elected patriarch, but this led to a split in the community, and, after his death in 1677, two separate patriarchs were elected. By 1702 the line of Syriac Catholic Patriarchs died out.

During the following century the Ottoman government supported the Eastern Orthodox community, including those related to the Patriarchate of Antioch. The Catholics were persecuted and during several periods the church was forced underground. In 1782 the Syriac Orthodox Holy Synod elected the Metropolitan of Aleppo as Patriarch Ignatius Mikhael III Jarwa; shortly afterward the patriarch declared himself Catholic and fled to Lebanon, where he built a monastery at Sharfeh. Since then, there has been an unbroken line of Syriac Catholic Patriarchs, each of whom has taken the additional name Ignatius.

After the Turkish government granted legal recognition to the Syriac Catholic Church the patriarchate moved back to Aleppo. But in the face of continued persecution and the massacres that took place during and after World War I, the patriarchate was moved first to Mardin in southern Turkey and eventually to Beirut, Lebanon.

Today the church fondly remembers Ignatius Cardinal Tabbouni, who served as patriarch for four decades and helped the church recover from the aftermath of World War II. Under his leadership the church became a community of strength and prosperity.

Educational opportunities for youth are a major strategy of the church, especially in dealing with continued emigration from the Middle East to the Americas, Europe, and Australia. The Ephremite Sisters, a congregation started in the 1960s, teach in several primary and secondary schools and care for dependent girls. In the diaspora, efforts are being made to maintain the church's identity by teaching the Syriac language. In the Mosul area of Iraq, several male clergy are following a semi-monastic discipline with priests of the Chaldean Catholic Church as they seek to promote lay education and parish renewal. The church maintains a publishing operation and a patriarchal seminary at the monastery in Sharfeh.

The ancient liturgy of Antioch is celebrated using a Western dialect of the classical Syriac language, but Arabic is used increasingly in parishes in the Middle East.

In some of the Christian towns and villages of eastern Syria and northern Iraq, where Syriac Catholics are numerous, modern Syriac is spoken in everyday life. (While it has been legal to speak Syriac in Iraq since the early 1970s, it is politically unpopular to do so today.) To the Oriental liturgies the church has added elements of Western Catholic piety, including the rosary and the stations of the cross.

LEADERSHIP

His Beatitude Patriarch Ignace Joseph III Younan, Patriarch of the
    Syriac Catholic Church of Antioch (b. 1944) (e. 2009)

CONTACT INFORMATION

Address: Syrian Catholic Patriarchate, Damascus Road, P.O. Box
    5087/116, Beirut, Lebanon

Tel.: +961.1.615.892

Fax: +961.1.616.573

E-mail: psc_lb@yahoo.com

Website: www.syriancatholic.org

MEMBERSHIP

The church claims a membership of 200,000 in the Middle East and the diaspora. The small size of the church is a direct result of the atrocities during and after World War I. Most Syriac Catholics belong to parishes related to dioceses in Lebanon, Syria, Iraq, and Egypt. Scattered parishes in Jerusalem, Jordan, the Sudan, and Turkey are each headed by a patriarchal vicar. In addition, a significant diaspora participates in parishes in Australia, the United States, Canada, and elsewhere in the West. The large Syro-Malankara Church in South India is historically related to the Syriac Catholic Church.

The Evangelical (Protestant) Family

An Introduction to the Evangelical Family

The Eastern churches did not experience the sixteenth-century Reformation that resulted in the great diversity of Protestant churches in the West; nor were they impacted by the religious fervor and mission movements of these churches until the early nineteenth century, when Western missionaries became active in the Middle East. Those who responded to the biblical teaching of the missionaries became known as *injiliyyeh* (pronounced in-jee-lee-ah), an Arabic term sometimes translated as "evangelists" and derived from the word for gospel or evangel. Some of these *injiliyyeh* were adherents of the historic Eastern churches who were impressed by the testimonies, personal devotion, and daily example of the men and women who had left their homelands to express their faith. The Protestants of the Middle East therefore became known as "Evangelicals," which does not refer to a conservative theology, as it does in the West, but to their response to the gospel.

Protestant mission societies brought with them a commitment to open schools and hospitals and to provide social services. These institutions have contributed greatly to the welfare of both Christians and Muslims in the Middle East. Unfortunately, the mission agencies also brought their own divisions, and the missionaries found it difficult to understand the ancient churches. In many cases, they were all too willing to begin new churches. Even though membership is small in numbers as compared to the ancient churches, the Protestant churches need to be discussed individually.

At the same time, these Protestant churches pioneered in ecumenism, beginning with the 1924 United Missionary Council in Jerusalem, the formation of the Near East Christian Council in 1956, and the Near East Council of Churches in 1964. When the Middle East Council of Churches was created in 1974, including the Oriental and Eastern Orthodox churches, the Evangelical churches recognized their need to continue developing unity among themselves. As a result they organized the Fellowship of the Middle East Evangelical Churches (FMEEC) to coordinate programs and activities.[1]

In the twentieth century, a new wave of mission activity began from Western churches and parachurch groups. Some of these groups have the goal of converting Muslims and/or Jews to the Christian faith while others seek to "convert" members of ancient churches. Many parachurch groups came to the Middle East with a heavy pro-Israeli agenda. Some remain very small, but others have tens of thousands of members.

The Middle East Council of Churches is challenged by the Evangelical churches that have not joined the MECC. This is partly because the non-Christian community has no way of distinguishing between the motives of each group, especially when some of the church groups side with the Israeli government against indigenous Christians and their ancient traditions. Organizations such as the Fellowship of the Middle East Evangelical Churches, the Protestant Community of Egypt, and the Supreme Council of the Evangelical Community in Syria and Lebanon form the entry point into ecumenical activity for these new, less ecumenical groups.

The Evangelical (Protestant) church family will be described below in two parts: members of the Middle East Council of Churches and non-members.

MEMBERS OF THE MIDDLE EAST COUNCIL OF CHURCHES

Eglise Reformée de France en Tunisie

Christianity came to North Africa in the early part of the Christian era, and during the third century Tunisia was an important Christian cen-

---

1. See pages 130-33 at the end of this chapter.

ter in the Roman Empire. From the capital city, Carthage, Christianity spread to other parts of North Africa and then into Europe during the next three centuries. Several prominent church teachers and leaders, including Tertullian, lived in Carthage; St. Augustine came from nearby Hippo. All that remains of that ancient church, however, is the literature it produced and the mosaic ruins of the churches and cemeteries. Some have said that the church of North Africa produced an incomparable elite but not an indigenous Christian people.

In the nineteenth century Western missionary agencies sought to reestablish Christianity where Islam had taken root. Churches were consequently constructed for the French- and English-speaking residents. In 1901 St. George's Church was built in Tunis on land that had served as a Christian cemetery since 1645. The worship and witness of this church continued uninterrupted during the two world wars. When Tunisia was a battlefield during World War II, the church distinguished itself as a center for Red Cross work.

Because the law prohibiting proselytism is rigidly enforced, very few native Tunisians belong to any of the churches in the country. Current ministries include education and social services. Worship is conducted largely in English and French.

LEADERSHIP
Pastor Lee de Hoog

CONTACT INFORMATION
Address: 36 rue Charles de Gaulle, Tunis, Tunisia
Tel. and Fax: +216.1.792.298

MEMBERSHIP
The Eglise Reformée de France en Tunisie is essentially an expatriate church and, as such, exists in Tunis and in several secondary cities that are year-round tourist centers.

Episcopal Church in Jerusalem and the Middle East

The Episcopal Church in Jerusalem and the Middle East is a province of the Worldwide Anglican Communion and covers the whole of the

Middle East. The earliest Anglican work in the Middle East is attributed to Henry Martyn, a chaplain for the East India Company who translated the New Testament into the three most important languages of the Muslim world. The more organized work can be attributed to the British Church Missionary Society (CMS) in Malta, Egypt, and Jerusalem.

The first Episcopal congregation was established in Iran among Armenians at New Julfa Isfahan in 1832. From 1841 to 1882 a combined Anglican/Lutheran bishopric was established jointly by the English and the Germans in Jerusalem. Although Anglican churches were formed with Palestinian clergy, English bishops continued to be appointed to the Middle East until 1958, when the Right Reverend Najib Kuba'an became the first Arab bishop of Jordan, Syria, and Lebanon. Soon thereafter the Archbishopric in Jerusalem was formed with dioceses serving Anglican churches in various parts of the Middle East. The careful designation of the bishop *in* Jerusalem was a sign of the respect that Anglicans have shown to the Orthodox churches and an unwillingness to suggest that the incumbent desired to usurp in any way the authority or standing of Eastern bishops and patriarchs. In 1976 the archbishopric was dissolved and the Episcopal Church in Jerusalem and the Middle East was created with four dioceses. All bishops are now elected by members of the national churches.

In addition to the ministries of the fifty-eight congregations and eight centers for occasional worship, the Episcopal Church operates hospitals, kindergartens, primary and secondary schools, a vocational school and orphanage, a home for the elderly, institutes for the deaf, a center for mentally handicapped persons, and bookshops and libraries. In the Holy Land, ministries to pilgrims are provided through St. George's Guest House in Jerusalem and St. Margaret's Hostel in Nazareth. St. George's College in Jerusalem is a center for fieldwork, study, and reflection, especially for visiting scholars.

The worship of the Episcopal Church generally follows the *Book of Common Prayer*, principally in Arabic and/or English as well as in Persian (Farsi) and other Asian languages.

LEADERSHIP
The Presiding Bishop (who heads the province)
The Most Rev. Dr. Munir Hanna Anis

CONTACT INFORMATION
Address: P.O. Box 87, Zamalek Distribution, 11211, Cairo, Egypt
Tel.: +20 (0)2 738 0821
Fax: +20 (0)2735 8941
E-mail: bishopmouneer@gmail.com
Website: www.dioceseofegypt.net

Diocesan bishops include:

BISHOP IN CYPRUS AND THE GULF
The Rt. Rev. Michael Augustine Owen Lewis
Address: P.O. Box 22075, CY1517, Nicosia, Cyprus
Tel.: +357 (0)22 671 220
Fax: +357 (0)22 672 241
E-mail: bishop@spidernet.com.cy
Website: www.cyprusgulf.anglican.org

BISHOP IN EGYPT WITH NORTH AFRICA AND THE HORN OF AFRICA
The Most Rev. Dr. Mouneer Hanna Anis
See contact information under Presiding Bishop

BISHOP IN IRAN
The Rt. Rev. Azad Marshall
Address: St. Thomas Center, Raiwind Road, P.O. Box 688, Lahore,
    Punjab, 54000, Pakistan
Tel.: +92 (0)42 542 0452
E-mail: bishop@saintthomascenter.org

BISHOP IN JERUSLEM
The Rt. Rev. Suheil Dawani
Address: St. George's Cathedral Close, Box 19122, Jerusalem, 91191,
    Israel
Tel.: +972 (0)2 627 1670
Fax: +972 (0)2 627 3847
E-mail: bishop@j-diocese.org
Website: www.j-diocese.org/

MEMBERSHIP

The province serves a small minority church with perhaps 30,000 members and affiliates. Congregations of the Jerusalem diocese are located in Israel and the West Bank and Gaza, and in Jordan, Syria, and Lebanon. The Diocese of Egypt with North Africa, Ethiopia, Somalia, Eritrea, and Djibouti also includes congregations in Algeria, Tunisia, and Libya. The Diocese of Cyprus and the Gulf includes congregations in Cyprus, Iraq, Yemen, and the Gulf States. Among the expatriates are many from eastern Asia. While there are indigenous congregations in Cyprus, Egypt, Iran, Jordan, Syria, and Israel/Palestine, many of the parishes serve English-speaking expatriates and some centers function as Protestant community churches.

Episcopal Church of the Sudan

Christianity first reached what is today the Sudan from Egypt and Ethiopia. By the sixth century, the Kingdom of Kush (in what is now the northern part of the Sudan) was considered Christian and the church was well established. With the spread of Islam, however, Christianity disappeared. The first modern expression of Protestantism has been credited to the Anglican bishop Llewellyn Gwynne, who began work in Omdurman in 1899. His efforts followed the invasion in 1898 by the Anglo-Egyptian expeditionary force that sought to extend British influence south from Egypt.

The colonial government tried to maintain the status quo in the northern part of Sudan but opened the southern area to missionary organizations. The effect of that "Southern Policy," together with the relative openness of the traditional religions and multiple cultures of the southern region, led to a rapid spread of Christianity. Schools and hospitals were allied with the church in this enterprise. Sudanese pastors and scores of trained lay catechists have played an important role in the church.

Until the 1950s, when the center of the church's life moved southward, the All Saints Cathedral in Khartoum stood as the center of British and Anglican activity. With the outbreak of civil strife in 1958 the church sought both to continue its educational ministry and to assist in meeting acute human needs. This witness has continued during the more than forty years of war in the country. Often the church and its members have suffered, but in this case the suffering has led to a stronger and growing church. The Episcopal Church in the Sudan was, until 1974, considered a part of the Anglican Archbishopric of Jerusalem. In 1976 it became a province with four dioceses, and by 2009 the province had 29 dioceses, each with its own bishop.

This church, like others that function in the southern Sudan, has sought to provide strong pastoral and spiritual care to the people of the region. It has played a major role in the distribution of humanitarian aid, especially to thousands of persons who have been displaced by the recurring civil strife. Relying in part on its global contacts with the Archbishop of Canterbury and the Anglican Consultative Council, the church frequently has been an advocate for the victims of violence who have no voice of their own. And, with the other churches in the country, the Episcopal Church of Sudan has sought to be a mediator and agent of reconciliation. Despite the major disruptions of the war, the church has sought to maintain its developmental and educational work.

The liturgy of the church is derived from the Anglican *Book of Common Prayer* and is conducted in Arabic, English, and several local languages.

LEADERSHIP
Dr. Daniel Deng Bul, archbishop of the Episcopal Church of the Sudan

CONTACT INFORMATION
Address: P.O. Box 110, Juba, Southern Sudan
Tel.: +249.811.200.40/5
Fax: +249.11.485.717
E-mail: archbishopdanieldeng@yahoo.com

MEMBERSHIP
The Episcopal Church of the Sudan is the second largest church in the Sudan with more than 5 million members. It is a province of the Worldwide Anglican Communion. An estimated 95 percent of the members live in the southern part of the Sudan. From 1983 to 1993, for example, the Diocese of Rumbeck grew from 9 to 357 congregations. In the north, there are Arabic-speaking parishes in Khartoum, Omdurman, Port Sudan, Wad Medani, and El Obeid, among other places.

Evangelical Church of Sudan, Now Called
Sudan Presbyterian Evangelical Church (SPEC)

The American Mission started in the northern part of Sudan as part of the Egypt-Sudan mission from the Presbyterian Church of North America. In 1964 all missionaries were expelled from the country, leaving the work of the mission in the hands of the Sudanese. The SPEC has grown in strength and numbers since that time, with congregations in all areas of northern and western Sudan.

The churches continued to thrive even though they were isolated from the rest of the church. Many churches are being re-established or rebuilt, and new congregations are being planted in these areas.

The SPEC is involved in a holistic ministry, including education for children, health work, literacy training for adults, and evangelism. The SPEC has a vision of working in the areas of the north where there is a strong Muslim presence and of planting churches in areas where there has been no Christian presence.

LEADERSHIP
Rev. Nagi Kunaji

CONTACT INFORMATION
P.O. Box 111019
Khartoum, Sudan
Tel.: +2249.83772158
E-mail: speckha@gmail.com

Evangelical Church of Egypt (Synod of the Nile)
(Sometimes called the
Evangelical Presbyterian Church of Egypt)

The Evangelical Church of Egypt (Synod of the Nile) is also known as The Synod of the Nile (Evangelical Church of Egypt). It was formerly known as the Coptic Evangelical Church, and sometimes as the Evangelical Presbyterian Church in Egypt. The result of missionary activity begun by the Prebyterians in 1853, it is in many ways the strongest Protestant church in the Middle East. The first Egyptian Presbyterian Council was formed in 1860 with seven members. Evangelical work spread quickly to

Alexandria and the Delta and then up the Nile to Asyut, where the first girls' school was formed in Upper Egypt. In 1899, the so-called Synod of the Nile sent a missionary pastor to the Sudan, where a church was formed in Khartoum in 1903. Until it became autonomous in 1958, the Synod of the Nile (with eight regional presbyteries) functioned as part of the general assembly of the Presbyterian Church (U.S.A.).

With strong Reformed theological beliefs, the Synod of the Nile began training Egyptian pastors through an Evangelical seminary that opened its doors just ten years after the first missionaries arrived. Another outgrowth of its Reformed theology was an emphasis on such social services as a hospital and several local medical centers, a broad educational program including literacy work (begun in 1930) and publishing, and development efforts. The latter emphasis led to the creation, in 1960, of the Coptic Evangelical Organization for Social Services (CEOSS), with a variety of ministries serving persons without regard to religious affiliation.

The church also has placed a major emphasis on evangelism, especially through the development of positive family relations and through many services to youth, including sports clubs, summer conferences, and local youth centers. The first youth organization was founded in 1916.

A total of twenty schools at all educational levels reach more than seventeen thousand boys and girls. In addition, there are vocational schools, including an advanced secretarial institute, and classes for mentally retarded girls. Local churches, in addition, operate thirty-seven private schools. The government has encouraged these programs. A well-equipped publishing house for Christian literature was developed in 1950 and the church has been a pioneer in the development of significant dialogue with Muslims despite the growth of Muslim extremism in Egypt.

The liturgy and spiritual life of the church is based on the Westminster Confession and on typical Presbyterian and Reformed patterns of worship.

LEADERSHIP

The president is elected for one year. At the time of this writing, the president is the Rev. Mohsen Moniur. The general secretary is the Rev. Refat Fathy.

CONTACT INFORMATION
Address: 402 Almiligi St., Elazbakeya, Cairo, Egypt; P.O. Box 1248
   Cairo 11221
Tel.: +202.25899920, or 25915448
Fax: +202.25918296
E-mail: epcegypt@yahoo.com

MEMBERSHIP
The Evangelical Presybyterian Church of Egypt includes 250,000 members and worshipers and more than 200 ordained Egyptian pastors as well as lay evangelists. Its 314 congregations, numerous preaching points, and various agencies are located throughout the Nile valley, from Alexandria to Aswan.

Evangelical Church of Iran

The Evangelical Church of Iran is partly the result of missionary work undertaken in 1832 by the American Board of Commissioners for Foreign Missions, representing the joint involvement of American Presbyterians and Congregationalists. Presbyterian missionaries at that time sought to revitalize and transform the local Nestorian church. (The Nestorian church resulted from a schism after the Third Ecumenical Council and emphasized the "divine" as the sole nature of Christ. When this teaching was banned in the Orthodox churches, the Nestorians fled to Persia.) The missionary efforts were rejected, possibly because they failed to understand the character of the historic church and because the Nestorians misunderstood the goals of the mission. In 1855, however, some of the Iranian Christians who were touched by the evangelical spirituality and witness left the Nestorian church, and seven Protestant congregations were organized in the region of Rezaiyeh in northwest Iran. The first presbytery was organized in 1862.

By the early 1930s there were eighteen congregations led by seven ordained pastors and several lay evangelists. In 1933 three presbyteries were organized and in 1971 these were redistributed along linguistic rather than geographical lines. The church was about 55 percent Assyrian, 21 percent Armenian, and the balance Persian and Jewish. Among the members were former Muslims, Jews, and followers of Zarathustra.

An independent synod, consisting of ordained and lay representatives, was formed in 1943 to serve all the Evangelical churches in Iran. In 1963 the churches approved a new constitution and today the synod includes three groups: the Armenian Evangelical Church, the Evangelical Presbyterian Church in Iran, and the Persian Evangelical Church.

Some of the historic educational and medical ministries of the church were closed by the government in 1979 at the time of the revolution. Several elementary schools, operated by individual congregations, presumably have been continued.

Worship styles include traditional Presbyterian elements, enriched and varied to meet local needs. Services are conducted in Armenian, Farsi, Turkish, and Syriac.

LEADERSHIP

The Moderator of the Synod is the Rev. Matauos Sergei Shaverdian

CONTACT INFORMATION

Address: P.O. Box 11365-4464, Tehran, Iran
Tel.: +98.21.674.095
Fax: +98.21.674.095

MEMBERSHIP

In the late 1980s there were forty-one congregations served by twelve ministers with an estimate of 3,100 members. The 2010 estimate is 1,500 members in 7 congregations. The congregations of what was formerly called the Evangelical Church in Iran are scattered across the northern part of the country.

Evangelical Lutheran Church in Jordan and The Holy Land (ELCJHL)

In 1841 an Anglo-Prussian joint bishopric was founded in Jerusalem with the intention of alternating bishops between the Anglicans and the Lutherans. The joint endeavor ended in 1886 but not before German deaconesses were invited to start a hospital, the forerunner of Augusta Victoria Hospital located on Jerusalem's Mount of Olives. Johann Ludwig Schneller joined with the German Lutherans to found an orphanage and several schools, some of which are still in existence. From 1886 until 1959 the Lutheran church in the Holy Land was led and headed by German missionaries.

The first Arab Lutheran congregation was organized in 1929 and others followed. Because these congregations were all in Jordanian territory when they formed a regional body, it was called the Evangelical Lutheran Church in Jordan and was officially recognized by King Hussein in 1959. Although that is still its legal name, the church goes by the name The Evangelical Lutheran Church in Jordan and The Holy Land. Following the 1967 war, five of the six Arab-speaking congregations were in the occupied West Bank. Since 1995, when the Israeli troops began their withdrawal from the occupied territories, the congregations in Beit Jala, Bethlehem, Beit Sahour, and Ramallah have been within the area administered by the Palestinian National Authority and, at this writing, re-occupied by Israel. Today the church is largely made up of refugees from 1948, many of whom fled from Lydda, Ramleh, and Jaffa. The first Palestinian bishop, the Right Reverend Daoud Haddad, was consecrated in 1979.

The major focus of ministry has been in the field of education, although a number of the churches pursue a variety of social services, including an international hostel. Five schools and two boarding homes have an enrollment of more than three thousand pupils, nearly half of whom are Muslim. Alternatives to mass tourism in the Holy Land have also developed as a concern, especially in Bethlehem and Jerusalem. Close relationships exist with other Lutheran endeavors in the area, including the Lutheran World Federation. In addition, Danish, Finnish, Swedish, and Norwegian Lutheran bodies maintain cooperative work in the Holy Land. There is also a close relationship between the ELCJHL and the international English-speaking congregation that is sponsored by the Evangelical Lutheran Church in America and worships in the Old City at Redeemer Lutheran Church.

The ELCJHL is developing the Dar Al-Kalima (House of the Word) Academy for interreligious and intercultural studies in Bethlehem and the International Center of Bethlehem, including a media center, under the direction of the Reverend Dr. Mitri Raheb.

Worship in the Arabic language follows traditional Lutheran forms and the church subscribes to the Augsburg Confession, which was translated into Arabic in 1993.

LEADERSHIP
The Rt. Rev. Munib Andria Younan, Bishop (b. 1950, e. 1996, c. 1998)

CONTACT INFORMATION
Address: Lutheran Church of the Redeemer , P.O. Box 14076,
    Muristan Road, Old City, Jerusalem, 91140
Tel.: +972.2.626680
Fax: +972.2.628.5764
E-mail: administration@elcjhl.org
Website: http://www.elcjhl.org

MEMBERSHIP
The Evangelical Lutheran Church in Jordan and The Holy Land has five congregations in the West Bank and one in Jordan with a total membership of nearly 3,000.

National Evangelical Church in Kuwait

Although it has only one parish, this church belongs to the Middle East Council of Churches as a member denomination. The first missionaries from the Reformed Church in America arrived in Kuwait at the beginning of the twentieth century. By 1909 Kuwaiti officials had agreed to permit the church to function freely.

The first congregation was made up of Christians who assisted in the mission. In 1926 the first prayer service in Arabic took place in the living room of the missionary family. Five years later, the first Protestant church was built; it was the first church to be built in the country. Prayer services were conducted in both Arabic and English every Sunday evening.

The first Arabic-speaking council of presbyters was elected in 1954 and the late Reverend Yusef Abdul-Nour became the first Arab pastor in 1959. Elders were elected to govern the church beginning in 1964. In 1966 the name of the church was changed from the Church of Christ to the National Evangelical Church in Kuwait.

The church provides worship and Bible study and offers the use of its buildings as the center for community life in the expatriate community. Services of worship and prayer follow the traditions of Reformed theology.

LEADERSHIP
Rev. Amanuel B. Y. Ghareeb

CONTACT INFORMATION
Address: P.O. Box 80, 13001 Safat, Kuwait
Tel.: +965.224.50307
Fax: +965.224.33230
E-mail: abghareeb@hotmail.com

MEMBERSHIP
One hundred and eighty persons are registered in the membership record of the National Evangelical Church in Kuwait located in Kuwait City.

National Evangelical Synod of Syria and Lebanon

The churches related to the National Evangelical Synod of Syria and Lebanon are the result of mission efforts from the United States and Europe that began about 1819. At that time, Presbyterian and Congregational teachers and pastors were sent by the American Board of Commissioners for Foreign Missions (ABCFM) to what became Syria and Lebanon. The joint effort continued until 1870 when, by agreement, the Presbyterian church assumed responsibility for activities in Greater Syria; the Congregationalists took over the work in Turkey.

Those who responded to the biblical teaching of the missionaries became known as "evangelists" (see the introduction above). Some of these "evangelists" kept their memberships in their traditional churches as they sought to base their lives on the Bible. Others organized themselves into separate congregations where the Scriptures were central. These churches came to be called "Evangelical churches." The first congregation was begun in Beirut in 1848 and the Ottoman Empire recognized the Protestant religion officially in 1850. Leadership in these early churches was characterized by the important role played by the laity, many of whom also were prominent in community affairs. One, Boutros Bustani, was a noted linguist who helped translate the Bible into Arabic, compiled the first Arabic encyclopedia, and helped establish the National School for Boys.

In 1920, when Syria and Lebanon became independent, a single synod was organized for the two countries. In 1959 the Synod assumed

---

Rev. Dr. Salim E. Sahiouny

When asked about his special role representing the Evangelical (Protestant) churches before the government, Dr. Salim E. Sahiouny, president of the Supreme Council of the Evangelical Community in Syria and Lebanon, replied, "I try to orient non-ecumenical churches so they will be more open to membership in the MECC." Because he represents the wide diversity of Protestant churches inside and outside the MECC, he is especially aware of those Evangelicals who do not cooperate with the council and the tensions that such groups often create.

Dr. Sahiouny received his Doctor of Ministry degree from McCormick Theological Seminary in Chicago, Illinois, and has held many positions in churches and religious organizations in the Middle East. His work has included being pastor in four local churches and general secretary of the National Evangelical Synod of Syria and Lebanon. He retired as general secretary of the Synod in 1995 to devote all of his time to the Supreme Council, of which he had become president in 1983. The Supreme Council is rooted in the *millet* system of the Ottoman Empire and is the body legally representing all Protestants. Today it represents non-conciliar Evangelical churches in addition to the principal Protestant denominations, and Dr. Sahiouny hopes that the Supreme Council's work will encourage all Protestants to work together in the future.

E-mail: suprcoun@minero.net

---

all educational, medical, and preaching responsibilities from the American Presbyterian Mission. In some places the transfer took place abruptly and the local congregational leaders were unable to carry full responsibility. As a result, a hospital and some of the schools (especially in Syria) became government institutions. In 1961 the National Evangelical Union was formed by a group of these churches that wanted to follow a different polity (namely, congregationalism).[2]

---

2. See the following section on the National Evangelical Union of Lebanon for further information.

In the 1970s, there was a strong movement of people from the villages to the cities and this demographic change led to larger urban congregations. Some redevelopment of the rural areas took place in the 1980s, leading to a revival in certain communities and churches. The lay committee structure of the church suffered during the seventeen-year civil war in Lebanon, and a major challenge since then has been the renewal of the infrastructure of the Synod and its churches. The church also launched a major program and rebuilt all its churches that were destroyed by war.

The Synod has continued the historic commitment of the Evangelical churches to the educational and human needs of the communities it serves. Its commitment to an educated clergy is demonstrated by its strong participation in the Near East School of Theology in Beirut. The churches in the Synod are deeply involved in the ecumenical movement, believing that they have something to contribute to and much to gain from the religious life they share with other Christians. Similarly, leaders of the Evangelical churches are prominent partners in the dialogue with Muslim neighbors. The philosophy of the Synod's diaconal work is to move beyond ecumenism to serve all humanity.

Arabic is used in the liturgy and preaching of the congregations related to the Synod. The worship normally follows the Reformed (Presbyterian) style with strong emphasis on congregational singing, thoughtful exposition of Scripture, and lay participation.

LEADERSHIP

The Rev. Fadi Dagher, General Secretary; The Rev. George Murad, Moderator

CONTACT INFORMATION

Address: Rabieh, Lebanon
Tel.: +961.4.411184
Fax: +961.4.411184
E-mail: nessl@synod-sl.org
Website: www.synod-sl.org
P.O. Box 70890 Antelias, Lebanon
Tel.: +961.4.525030

MEMBERSHIP

The 58 congregations, with a membership of 20,000, are the major Evangelical community in Syria and Lebanon.

National Evangelical Union of Lebanon

In numerous ways, the National Evangelical Union reflects the gradual maturing of mission theology. At the beginning of the nineteenth century two U.S. denominations, the Congregationalists and Presbyterians, agreed to unite their work through the American Board of Commissioners for Foreign Missions (ABCFM). Together they brought the Reformation message to the Middle East. Records of the first preaching service in what is today Lebanon show that in 1823 these missionaries were aware of the historic churches in the region and that their policy was not to establish a local church but to refer any converts from Islam and Judaism to nearby Orthodox churches. When Christians from the traditional churches came to these missionaries, they were urged to work for renewal within their own communities of faith.

By 1847, however, a small group of Lebanese who worked with the missionaries as teachers desired their own church in Beirut, petitioning the missionaries to permit them to conduct their own services in Arabic. They called their little congregation the Native Evangelical Church and later the National Evangelical Church of Beirut; in both instances they meant to imply "not American." Several other congregations were formed in Mount Lebanon and in several parts of Syria. In 1870 they built their first church building to be used by both the Lebanese and the Anglo-American congregations, at about the same time that the ABCFM transferred responsibility for the mission field in Syria and Lebanon to the Presbyterian mission board. In the early years, Arabic-speaking missionaries led worship, but in 1890 they called the Reverend Yusuf Badr, a Lebanese Presbyterian, as the first full-time pastor.

By 1958 the new understanding of mission led the missionaries to serve as fraternal workers within a self-governing church. By that time the National Evangelical Church of Beirut already was functioning as an independent body that decided to follow congregational rather than Presbyterian polity.

As Beirut began to develop as an economic and cultural center, vil-

---

Ms. Jean Zaru

Jean Zaru is a Christian and a Palestinian; she is also an outspoken peace activist. For five generations, her family has lived in Ramallah, where from the fifteenth century until very recently the majority of residents were Christian. Jean clearly remembers the anguish of the refugees from the 1948 and 1967 wars. She is a Quaker and has been active in the local and international YWCA as well as the World Council of Churches. She is also a founding member of the Sabeel Ecumenical Liberation Theology Center in Jerusalem.

Ms. Zaru has spoken on peace and the Middle East in forums and meetings around the world and engages in dialogue with people of all religions who are trying to work nonviolently. She stresses that you cannot bring about peace and security through violence of any kind. At the 2001 World Council of Churches consultation on the Israeli-Palestinian issue she stressed that "Occupation is violence, and in the Decade to Overcome Violence, we have to expose the structural violence of occupation."

(Quotation taken from the MECC
NewsReport, Summer 2001, p. 30.)

---

lagers came to the city and the National Evangelical Church of Beirut grew substantially. A number of scattered congregations looked to the larger church in Beirut as their leader and, after Presbyterian congregations organized the National Evangelical Synod of Syria and Lebanon,[3] these congregational churches in 1961 established the National Evangelical Union.

The members of the Union seek to make an ecumenical witness, demonstrating their concern for the entire Christian community and for all the people of Lebanon. They are deeply involved in a home for orphans and in vocational and academic education. Their commit-

3. See the previous section on the National Evangelical Synod of Syria and Lebanon for further information.

ment to theological education is demonstrated by their role in the founding and continued development of the Near East School of Theology. Much of the church and school property in Beirut belonging to the Union was destroyed during the long civil war. Only the tower of the downtown church was left standing. That tower has been incorporated into a new, contemporary building as a reminder of the violence and hatred that war creates. The National Evangelical Union of Lebanon is seeking by its participation in the Beirut renaissance to respond to new opportunities that God is offering today throughout the society. The liturgy, with its emphasis on preaching, is in Arabic.

LEADERSHIP
The Rev. Dr. Habib Badr, Presiding Pastor (b. 1950, e. 1985)

CONTACT INFORMATION
Address: P.O. Box 11-5224, Beirut, Lebanon
Tel.: +961.1.980051/2
Fax: +961.1.980.050
E-mail: nec.Beirut@t-net.com
Website: www.nechurchbeirut.org

MEMBERSHIP
The total membership of the nine congregations, four of which are especially active, is estimated at about 6,000 adults and children, with congregations in Beirut and its suburbs and in the nearby mountains.

Presbyterian Church of the Sudan (PCOS)

Presbyterian and Reformed missionaries, many of whom died of malaria in the early years, began efforts in the remote areas of southern Sudan in 1902. From the beginning, educational work, including the training of pastors and teachers, was among their efforts. In 1948 the churches were formed into a presbytery of the Synod of the Nile (Evangelical Church of Egypt) and became the independent Church of Christ in the Upper Nile in 1956. The name was later changed to the Presbyterian Church of the Sudan. All missionaries were forced to leave in 1964, but since 1956 the Sudanese leaders have functioned with full autonomy.

The church has grown rapidly, especially in the latter part of the long civil war. One pastor, for example, in the first year of his ministry, baptized 9,288 persons. Although many of the ministers have had only minimal training, their theological commitment is that the church exists for all the people and that the gospel teaches repentance and forgiveness as essential to the process of reconciliation so urgently needed in the badly divided nation. The church accepts cultural, linguistic, and social diversity as a gift of God and seeks to carry out its ministry in a variety of languages.

Like other Sudanese Christian denominations, the church must cope with the division between the north and south of Sudan, and a large number of refugees and displaced persons. The PCOS operates schools, health clinics, and other needed services within the camps for displaced persons, along with a mission and evangelism department. It is hoped with the upcoming vote on whether or not to divide Sudan into two countries, things will settle down and the needs of the church will change.

Worship — in Arabic, English, and local languages — is derived from Reformed and Presbyterian liturgies introduced by missionaries from the United States.

LEADERSHIP
Rev. Peter Makwac

CONTACT INFORMATION
Address: P.O. Box 3421, Khartoum, Sudan
Tel.: +249.11.445.1148
E-mail: pcos.malakal2007@yahoo.com

MEMBERSHIP
The Presbyterian Church in the Sudan is the third largest Christian community in the Sudan, being organized with 250 congregations in nine parishes. There are an estimated 600,000 members, in the southern part of the Sudan. The congregations are served by seventy-two pastors and twelve lay evangelists, many of whom are self taught and most of whom receive no salaries from the churches.

Protestant Church of Algeria

The first Protestants to settle in Algeria in modern times belonged to the French Protestant Church. They arrived shortly after France occupied Algeria in 1830, and they served French-speaking settlers. A group of Lutherans served newcomers from Alsace-Lorraine. Among those who became active in North Africa in the latter part of the nineteenth century were Methodist missionaries from the United States who succeeded in beginning a small community of under four hundred members. A few of these Methodists lived across the eastern border of Algeria in Tunisia. Others who arrived were small groups representing the Salvation Army, Baptists, Mennonites, Adventists, Anglicans, Plymouth Brethren, and numerous Pentecostal groups. Since none of the latter groups maintained a mission in Algeria, those who remained were gradually assimilated into the French Reformed or Methodist groups.

During the colonial period the French Reformed Church in Algeria was an integral part of the Reformed Church of France. Its members were settlers engaged in agriculture, commerce, education, or civil service. Since its primary service was to those members, its growth was most significant within that population. Other Protestant groups, including the Methodists, developed programs for various language groups.

When Algeria won its independence in 1962, the French Reformed Church became autonomous. The Methodists, however, maintained their connectional structure with the U.S. General Conference. Many French members of both churches returned to France, while others remained in Algeria, some opting for Algerian citizenship. Membership continued to decline, especially in times of turmoil. By 1972 it became evident to church leaders that the various Protestant churches would fare better united than as weak denominations. Consequently, in that year, the Eglise Protestante d'Algerie was formed by bringing together Methodists, Reformed, the Salvation Army, Mennonites, and remnants of the Assemblies of God. At the peak of the church, its members represented forty nationalities and it served 20 percent of all Christians in the country. It has continued to maintain strong ecumenical ties both within and without the country. The worship of this church follows Reformed, Methodist, and other patterns of worship. French and Arabic are the principal languages.

LEADERSHIP
The Rev. Hugh Johnson

CONTACT INFORMATION
Address: 31 Rue Reda Hou Hou, Alger, Algeria
Tel.: +071503048 or 070689889

MEMBERSHIP
The Protestant Church of Algeria (Eglise Protestante d'Algerie) includes persons with backgrounds in many different church traditions,
speaking a couple dozen national languages. Many are expatriates living throughout Algeria. Church membership has continued to decline
in recent years. The church's existence, at a time when there is a strong
militant Islamic movement, is precarious and difficult.

Sudan Presbyterian Evangelical Church (SPEG)
See **Evangelical Church of Sudan** (p. 108).

Union of Armenian Evangelical
Churches in the Near East

The churches that participate in this Union represent the traditions of
both the Protestant Reformation and the Armenian Apostolic
Church. Deeply rooted in the Armenian nation, these Evangelical
churches began in 1846 as a reforming movement within the mother
church. They were the result of contacts with missionaries from the
United States who worked in Turkey under the American Board of
Commissioners for Foreign Missions (then Presbyterian and Congregational).

The early members of the Armenian Evangelical churches in Turkey were excommunicated from the Armenian Orthodox Church when
they rejected a new "creed" formulated by their patriarch. They pre-
ferred to state that "the true foundation and perfect rule of Christian
faith is the Holy Scriptures alone" and that they had "received" the historic Nicene Creed. Following the establishment of the first congregation in what is now Istanbul, membership grew to more than sixty-five

thousand with ninety pastors in Turkey alone. The massacres of Armenians in the early part of the twentieth century led to the death or dispersion of nearly all Armenians. Like the Apostolic Church, the Armenian Evangelical Church developed congregations among refugees in and around Beirut, on the Syrian border, and in Damascus and Aleppo. The Union was formed in 1923.

It is a measure of the strength of the Armenian peoples that close relationships are maintained not only with the Evangelical diaspora but also with the Apostolic Catholicosate of Cilicia and with the Armenian Catholic Patriarchate.

The Union and its member churches are known for their commitment to youth and especially to education. Many of the congregations have day schools that range from kindergarten to the secondary level as well as Sunday schools and youth organizations. In Lebanon, the Union owns the Haigazian University, which publishes the *Armenological Review* of scholarly papers, and a social action center that helps needy families and individuals with medical and other forms of assistance. With sister Protestant churches, the Union co-sponsors the Near East School of Theology (see page 181). In cooperation with members of the Armenian Apostolic Church, the Union operates a home for the elderly, a home for the blind, and a school for slow-learning children. In addition, there is a jointly operated sanitarium in Lebanon, and a home for the elderly in Aleppo, Syria, is sponsored by the three Armenian denominations.

The liturgical language of these churches is Armenian. The worship follows Reformed traditions, enriched by liturgical elements shared with the Armenian mother church. Sermons generally are presented in Arabic or a local language.

LEADERSHIP
Rev. Megrdich Karagoezian, President

CONTACT INFORMATION
Address: Ibrahim Bacha Street, Mar Michael, P.O. Box 110377, Beirut, Lebanon
Tel.: +961.1.443.547 and 565.628
Fax: +961.1.565.629
E-mail: uaecne@cyberia.net.lb
Website: http://www.uaecne.org

MEMBERSHIP

The twenty-five autonomous Armenian Evangelical congregations that together form this Union are located in Lebanon, Syria, Turkey, Egypt, and Iran, with one church in Athens, Greece. (There are similar unions of Armenian evangelicals in France, North America, Armenia, Georgia, and Bulgaria.) Estimated membership is 9,500.

NON-CONCILIAR CHURCHES (NON-MEMBERS OF THE MIDDLE EAST COUNCIL OF CHURCHES)

Very few of these churches have offices or denominational headquarters in the Middle East. Many are the result of twentieth-century missionary work, and they rely on headquarters in other countries. Contacts in the Middle East are listed when available. The congregations are generally autonomous.

Armenian Evangelical Spiritual Brotherhood

This community, sometimes known as the Armenian Brethren, began in Aleppo, Syria, in 1920 as an association of persons who withdrew from the Armenian Orthodox, Armenian Catholic, and Armenian Evangelical churches. Very small congregations are located in Syria, Lebanon, Egypt, Iraq, and Iran. Members are known for their close-knit and pietistic way of life. Lay leadership is important, as they have no ordained clergy. A committee of elders elected by the congregation administers each congregation independently.

Assemblies of God

Autonomous Assemblies of God churches, located in Egypt, Israel, Jordan, and Lebanon, are the result of missionary activity by the American pentecostal denomination of the same name. The churches emphasize the power of the Holy Spirit to change lives and the participation of all members in the work and witness of the church. More than 170 congregations have been organized in Egypt, where nearly 150,000 baptized members support an orphanage in Asyut. There is also a small postnatal clinic in a poor section of Cairo. In Israel, where there are twelve congregations and twenty preaching points, there are now about five hundred members. In Lebanon a presidential decree gave the Evangelical Assemblies of God the right to establish churches, schools, orphanages, a drug ministry, and a Bible correspondence school. Bible schools and correspondence study are offered in Arabic and English in each country, and, in Israel, also in Russian. In addition, the Galilee Bible College is located in Haifa, Israel. Some work is being undertaken in other countries including those in the Persian Gulf area.

LEADERSHIP
Doug Clark is an area director.

CONTACT INFORMATION
Address: Assemblies of God Middle East and North Africa, P.O. Box
    25749, 1311 Nicosia, Cyprus
Tel.: +357.2.267.3004
Fax: +357.2.267.0524
E-mail: servant@logos.cy.net

Baptist Churches

About 80 autonomous Baptist churches are located in the Middle East with a variety of missionary origins. Those historically related to the Southern Baptist Convention, U.S.A., are located in Lebanon and Jordan with smaller groups in Egypt, Iraq, Turkey and Palestine/Israel. They maintain elementary and secondary schools, programs in refugee camps in Palestine, a hospital in Jordan, Bible correspondence courses, an extensive radio ministry, and a pastoral ministry to expatriates in the Arabian peninsula. Their work began in the 1940s. An Arab Baptist Theological Seminary is located in Mansourieh near Beirut. Various groups of Baptists also are involved in the Bethlehem Bible College in Palestine.

Christian Brethren

Informally and locally organized, Christian Brethren groups are difficult to number but are significant in many places, especially Egypt. It is likely that there are at least seven thousand members. There also are local fellowships in Turkey, Iran, Cyprus, Lebanon, and Palestine/Israel. There are expatriate groups in Tunisia, Morocco, Saudi Arabia, Kuwait, and South Yemen. Related to the Plymouth Brethren from England and the United States, the Christian Brethren have roots in Anabaptist and evangelical theologies, observe the Lord's Supper weekly, and stress evangelism and missionary activity.

Church of God

The Church of God (Anderson, Indiana, U.S.A.) has congregations in Turkey, Lebanon, Syria, Jordan, Cyprus, and Egypt, where a bookshop is maintained. The first work in the region began in Egypt in 1912 and quickly spread to Lebanon and Jordan. Like the mother church in the United States, the parishes in the Middle East are strongly influenced by Wesleyan theology and pietism with attention being given to conversion, holiness, Bible study, and hymn singing. More than thirteen churches have been organized in Egypt, where nearly twelve hundred members are active. A unique Church of God fellowship in Cairo serves some one hundred adults and children who retain their ties with Coptic Orthodox and Armenian congregations. Across the Mediterranean region there are more than two thousand members in about thirty congregations. In both Egypt and Lebanon there are active national organizations known as Assemblies; each has a local chairperson who serves on a rotating basis. Extensive programs of evangelism among youth are a special emphasis of these churches, which are also served by the Mediterranean Bible College in Beirut. The churches are independent but are generally resourced by missionaries.

Church of the Nazarene

This international church has its headquarters in Kansas City, Missouri, in the United States, and has some twenty relatively small congregations in Turkey, Cyprus, Egypt, Jordan, Lebanon, Syria, and Palestine/Israel. The general theological emphasis of the members is on the importance of a devout and holy life and a positive witness of the power of the Holy Spirit. The church operates schools and youth programs in Jordan, Lebanon, and Palestine/Israel and has an estimated 831 members. The first missionaries of the Church of the Nazarene in the region were sent in 1920. The church maintains an Eastern Mediterranean Field Office in Jerusalem.

LEADERSHIP
Lindell Browning is the field director

CONTACT INFORMATION
Address: P.O. Box 19426, Jerusalem, via Israel
Tel.: +972.2.671.5080
Fax: +972.2.582.1172
E-mail: EMFO@netvision.net.il

Churches of Christ

Churches of Christ missionaries from the United States began work in Lebanon in 1961, establishing three churches and opening a Bible Training School in Beirut. Members of the church believe that the Bible alone determines matters of faith and practice. Their literature and Bible correspondence program was extended to Egypt, Syria, Jordan, and Israel/Palestine, where there is one expatriate congregation in Jerusalem and two indigenous congregations in Nazareth and the Galilee. There also is an expatriate congregation in Tripoli, Libya.

Christian Alliance Churches

Local churches begun through the efforts of the U.S.-based Christian and Missionary Alliance are located in Lebanon, Syria, and Jordan. Today they are part of two parallel groups, the Christian Alliance Church of Lebanon and Syria (whose president lives in Damascus) and the Christian Alliance Church of Jordan (whose president resides in Amman). A congregation in Jerusalem, related to the Church of Jordan, has been largely isolated by the political situation.

The first Alliance work began in 1890 when two female missionaries were sent to Jerusalem. Other missionaries soon went elsewhere in the region. A high priority was to open churches in Arabia, and at one point the mission was called the Palestine and Northern Arabian Border Mission. The missionaries were never able to enter Arabia, however, and finally concentrated their work elsewhere.

Today there are there are five congregations in Lebanon with an inclusive membership of 546, seventeen congregations in Syria with a total membership of 1,535, and seven congregations in Jordan with 824 members. The Alliance churches maintain the Christian Alliance Institute of Theology in Beirut, which offers a four-year B.A. degree. Students come from the three countries and also from Egypt, the Sudan, and Iraq. A missionary nurse from this church was killed in Sidon, Lebanon, in 2002 by Muslim extremists who claimed she had been proselytizing.

LEADERSHIP
The field director for the area is Darrell Phenicie. The C&MA headquarters are in Colorado Springs, Colorado.

CONTACT INFORMATION
E-mail: Darrell.Phenicie@nyack.edu

Free Methodist Church

A growing Egyptian community of Free Methodists is the result of missionary work by North Americans who did not engage themselves elsewhere in the region. There are more than seventy congregations of about fifty persons each in various cities and towns along the Nile. Members agree to live simply, worship regularly, and practice daily devotions and responsible stewardship. Their advocacy of the rights of all persons has appealed especially to the poor and oppressed.

Messianic Jews

A small but rapidly growing group of Israeli Jews has voluntarily decided to embrace a faith in Jesus (Yeshua) of Nazareth as Son of God, personal Redeemer and Messiah. They reject being considered "converts to Christianity" but consider themselves as "completed Jews." Their generally vital congregations meet without public fanfare because of laws prohibiting proselytism. These congregations emphasize attachment to Jewish heritage and Jewish national characteristics. In fifty years their numbers have increased dramatically, almost exclusively by personal invitation or word of mouth. It is estimated that there may be as many as five to eight thousand members who are located in the major cities of Israel. The Caspari Center in Jerusalem is a contact point for this group.

Religious Society of Friends (Quakers)

This group has small but active "meetings" in Israel/Palestine, Lebanon, and elsewhere. The Friends are noted as peace activists and as advocates for minority and human rights. They sponsor primary and secondary schools. Lay leadership is important for the meetings and individual members of this group often are active in ecumenical affairs. (See Jean Zaru, page 118.)

Seventh-day Adventists

This international church, which has its central office in Silver Spring, Maryland, U.S.A., maintains a Middle East Division with nearly fifty churches in Egypt, Lebanon, Iraq, Iran, Palestine/Israel, Jordan, Cyprus, Turkey, and the southern Sudan. The church has a Middle Eastern membership of several thousand, the largest numbers being in Egypt and Lebanon. Members look forward to the second advent of Christ, worship on Saturday, and maintain an energetic missionary program. In the Middle East they have secondary schools in Egypt, Jordan, and Lebanon, a Middle East College and press in Lebanon, as well as food processing plants, orphanages, and correspondence school programs in several countries.

BRIDGING THE DENOMINATIONAL BARRIERS

While the Eastern Orthodox Churches already see themselves as an international federation, the patriarchs of the Oriental Orthodox family meet together annually to affirm their unity and theology. The Catholic family of churches is bound together by allegiance to the Vatican and a region-wide Catholic conference of bishops, but the Evangelical (Protestant) Churches have no such official ties to each other. They continue to draw strength from each other through an organization known as the Fellowship of the Middle East Evangelical Churches (FMEEC). This organization brings together fifteen Reformed, Lutheran, and Episcopal churches[4] from Algeria and Tunisia in the West to Iran in the East, from Syria and Lebanon in the north to the Gulf and the Sudan in the south.

Many of the churches that work together in the fellowship are also active in what is the most inclusive ecumenical organization in the world — the Middle East Council of Churches. The MECC, in fact, developed from the largely Protestant Near East Council of Churches, which had its own roots in the collaborative efforts of missionaries in the region beginning in 1924. The NECC was officially formed in 1962, drawing the Protestant churches together for common witness. Almost immediately those Protestant churches reached out to the historic churches in the region and that led to the birth of the Middle East Council of Churches.[5]

As Roseangela Jarjour, the general secretary of FMECC, describes the spirit of the fellowship, "The evangelical church, through its biblical concepts and spirituality, yearns for unity." This yearning does not

---

4. These fifteen churches are the Evangelical Church of Egypt, the Episcopal Church in Egypt, the National Evangelical Synod of Syria and Lebanon, the Union of the Armenian Evangelical Churches in the Near East, the National Evangelical Union of Lebanon, the Episcopal Church in Iran, the Evangelical Church of Iran, the Episcopal Church in Jerusalem and the Middle East, the Evangelical Lutheran Church in Jordan and the Holy Land, the Episcopal Church in Cyprus and the Gulf, the National Evangelical Church in Kuwait, the Episcopal Church of the Sudan, the Presbyterian Church of the Sudan, the Sudan Presbyterian Evangelical Church, and the Protestant Church of Algeria.

5. See "The Churches of the Middle East Now Work Together," pp. 22-31 in this volume.

mean that the member churches within FMEEC are fully united. Theological questions related to Eucharist and the nature of ministry are still unsolved, so the quest for unity is a top priority for the FMEEC, which believes that unity among its members will foster the unity with the other churches. In 1997 FMEEC formulated a "Proposal for the Unity of the Evangelical Churches in the Middle East," which was not accepted by all its members. A new proposal was launched in 2005, leading to the "Agreement of Full Mutual Recognition between the Lutheran and Reformed Churches in the Middle East and North Africa." That Agreement was formally signed in 2006.[6]

In a May 2002 speech, the General Secretary described the activities of the FMEEC. They are trying

- to bring the member churches closer to unity through working and learning together;
- to rebuild a generation of leaders in churches that were depleted by wars and emigration;
- to develop a core group of women and men for the churches and for the ecumenical movement in a region where the churches have not seriously sought to strengthen lay leadership — a region that is patriarchal, hierarchical, and clerical;
- to build a new leadership base that is better educated, more ecumenically oriented, and possesses more leadership skills.[7]

The fellowship believes that these goals require major efforts in the area of theology. Through a program that engages laymen and laywomen, the FMEEC seeks to increase an understanding of the Evangelical identity and heritage shared by the churches and to encourage the member churches to grow more closely together. The churches have undertaken this effort specifically to coordinate their positions on the issues currently being discussed in the wider ecumenical forum. "We

6. In a variety of ways each of the four families of churches is working within its own tradition and bilaterally on the "church-dividing issues." It is fair to say that in their "dialogue of life" with Muslims, the historic divisions in the Christian church are difficult to explain and are perceived by Muslims as a sign of weakness.

7. From the text of a speech by Roseangela Jarjour prepared for delivery to the May 2002 Convention of the U.S.-based organization Evangelicals for Middle East Understanding held near Beirut, Lebanon.

have a vision of a specific role that we can play as Evangelicals in the Middle East," Ms. Jarjour says. "We have something to contribute as Protestants to other Christians as well as to non-Christians here in the region."

The FMEEC churches work closely with Evangelical seminaries in Beirut and Cairo; they sponsor research, conferences, and conversations on intellectual and theological issues; they offer practical and theological seminars for pastors; and they publish books and articles by Evangelical scholars from the region. A related program effort is specifically geared to women, developing a network of Evangelical women across the Middle East, seeking to strengthen the role of women in the churches and in the society, and establishing a theological base for the ministries of women, including pastors' wives. Theological training seminars are organized especially for young women.

The fellowship provides a continuing theological and practical program offering a curriculum of 12 courses, covered in three years, for use with the children, young people, and families in Sunday schools. Another focus is the production of resources in Arabic to be used as educational aids for various age groups. Eighteen episodes of a DVD program called "Stream of Thoughts" have been produced for ages 18 to 25. A manual for youth leaders also is available.

The Evangelical churches in the Middle East have pioneered in general education, seeking to communicate Christian values without compromising high academic standards. The church-sponsored schools have, in fact, helped to establish an appreciation for quality education. The fellowship helps the churches continue their schools and collaborates with the universities that share historical ties to the member churches by offering training especially for the schools' headmasters. FMEEC encourages the schools to continue their work in academic research and logical reasoning as essential to freedom of thought, openness to others, and the practice of democracy.

In the last several years the fellowship has provided theological and practical training for pastors and laypersons of the churches of Iran, Iraq, and Sudan. The training is designed to strengthen the witness and ministry of the churches with youth and women, in evangelism and in Sunday schools. A meeting of the FMEEC in December 2009 unanimously approved the ordination of women as pastors.

During and following the Ottoman Empire the *millet* system was established by which churches had to form organizations to provide standing before the government and to resolve their own internal legal issues.[8] The Protestant *millets* still exist in a modified form as a way of relating to the government as a group of churches. One such group is called the Supreme Council of the Evangelical Community in Syria and Lebanon. In Egypt there is a similar organization called the Protestant Community of Egypt. Neither sees itself in competition with the FMEEC.

FMEEC LEADERSHIP
Ms. Rosangela Jarjour, General Secretary

FMEEC CONTACT INFORMATION
Address: P.O. Box 213, Ain Arr, Lebanon
Tel.: + 961 3 713009
Fax: + 961 4 919126
E-mail: fmeec-gs@cytanet.com.cy; fmeec@fmeec.org

8. See the boxed text on p. 54 for a fuller description of the *millet* system.

The Assyrian Church of the East

The Assyrian Church of the East is one of the oldest Christian communities, tracing its origins to the witness of St. Thomas and other apostles in ancient Mesopotamia. In the early fourth century (between A.D. 300 and 310), bishops of the church were organized under a catholicos who was bishop of the Persian royal capital, Seleucia-Ctesiphon. Poor political relations between Byzantium and Persia in the fourth and fifth centuries produced dire consequences for the Church of the East. The faithful already were suspect as collaborators with Christians in the Roman Empire, especially after the Edict of Milan in 313. Motivated by a sincere desire to resolve the ongoing difficulties occasioned by the church's putative relationship to the West and not by hostility, a synod was called in 499. By canonical decree, the bishops proclaimed the Church of the East to be administratively autocephalous from the "Western" bishops, and enhanced the power and dignity of the catholicos, adding the title of patriarch.

This administrative separation from the Western bishops is notable for its lack of a theological cause of schism. Although the break later caused the Orthodox to call the church "Nestorian," there were no doctrinal or conciliar issues involved at the time, for the separation took place prior to the Council of Ephesus and four years prior to Nestorius's appointment to the See of Constantinople. On the contrary, the tone of the canons of the synod was laudatory and sincerely affectionate and grateful for the past help from Western bishops. That said, it is also true that the Church of the East only accepts the first two ecumenical councils and that it holds the doctrine of the separation of the two natures of Christ. The other churches considered this heretical.

From the sixth to the thirteenth centuries, the Church of the East was a vibrant missionary church. According to some historians, it was geographically, and possibly demographically, the largest Christian community in the world, extending from Cyprus in the West to China in the Far East, reaching to India, Tibet, and Mongolia. During this period the Church of the East became known for its contribution to Arab culture through scholarly activity — including institutional education and translation of Greek philosophy — centering in the schools of Edessa and Nisibis and later at the schools of Jundi-shapur and Baghdad.

During the fourteenth century, however, the church was again persecuted, and was virtually annihilated during the march of Tamerlane. In the twentieth century, the Assyrians (like the Armenians) suffered persecutions in what is now eastern Turkey. Most of the survivors fled to Iraq only to face massacre and deportation again.

Because of theological positions it took in the fifth and sixth centuries, communion was broken between the Church of the East and the church of the Roman Empire. Having survived brutal persecutions, the church was weak when Dominican and Franciscan missionaries began work in the region in the thirteenth century. Prompted by internal conflicts (in part due to a debate over rights of certain families to hereditary succession to the patriarchal and episcopal sees), a number of bishops of the Church of the East, said to be "disposed" toward the Catholic Church, eventually sought recognition by Pope Julius III, and a separate Chaldean Catholic Church was formed in 1553.

In 1978 the catholicos-patriarch took up residence in the United States. By 1994 the Assyrian Holy Synod had decided to reach out to other churches and a historic event took place in that year when Patriarch Mar Dinkha IV and Pope John Paul II signed a "Common Christological Declaration." The declaration noted that "the controversies of the past led to anathemas, bearing on persons and on formulas. The Lord's Spirit permits us to understand better today that the divisions brought about in this way were due in large part to misunderstandings." So, the statement adds, "we experience ourselves united today in the confession of the same faith in the Son of God who became man so that we might become children of God by his grace." The declaration affirmed the opportunity to witness together "to the Gospel message and [to cooperate] in particular pastoral situations, including especially the areas of catechesis and the formation of future priests."

In the same year, the sixth assembly of the MECC agreed that the ancient Assyrian Church of the East should be admitted to full membership, within the Catholic family. The church chose not to join the council, however, and it is still not a member of the Middle East Council of Churches. Nevertheless, it has not abandoned ecumenical contacts. In 1997, after years of personal contacts and collaboration, the Assyrian and Chaldean Holy Synods signed a "Joint Synodal Decree for Promoting Unity" and established a "Joint Commission for Unity." Such collaborations will greatly assist the scattered Assyrian Church.

The church places a high priority on the education of children and youth, and seeks to preserve the ethnic and spiritual traditions of the Assyrian people. Church leaders give considerable attention to theological dialogue and relations with other Christian bodies.

The worship of the Assyrian Church is primarily in the Eastern dialect of classical Syriac (Aramaic) and is traced to the ancient liturgies of Edessa. The Liturgy of the Holy Apostles is one of the oldest forms of worship used anywhere today. It dates from the early fourth century and is also thought to preserve elements of Persian rites that have been lost for centuries. The preparation of the Eucharist includes the "holy leaven," or *Malka,* which is a piece of dough that is kept from one baking to another, symbolizing continuity with the Last Supper, when the Apostle John is said to have kept a piece of bread.

The Assyrian Church uses neither icons nor images; the simple interior of the churches includes a stand on which a cross and the Gospels are placed.

LEADERSHIP

His Holiness Khanania Mar Dinkha IV, Catholicos-Patriarch of the
    Church of the East (b. 1935, e. 1976)

CONTACT INFORMATION

Address: 8908 Birch Avenue, Morton Grove, Illinois, 60053, U.S.A.
Tel.: +847.966.0617
Fax: +847.966.0012
Website: www.cired.org

MEMBERSHIP

The church estimates its current worldwide membership at about 400,000 with bishoprics in Iraq, Syria, Iran, Lebanon, India, Australia and New Zealand, Europe, and North America. Emigration from the Middle East continues, partly because of the economic appeal of North America and Australia and partly because of persecution. Members are deeply loyal to their church and to their ethnic origins even though the catholicos-patriarch resides in North America. Their claim to Assyrian nationality has led to frequent persecution, and in some countries young people are not permitted to serve in the military or certain sensitive vocations.

PART III

CHURCH AND STATE
IN THE MIDDLE EAST

A Brief History

For most Western Christians, some form of separation between religion and government is taken for granted. Even where there are established religions, as in the United Kingdom, there is a significant distinction between church and state. Efforts in Russia to limit religious groups other than the Russian Orthodox Church have focused attention on this issue. In the United States disagreements have led to controversies over prayer in schools and the teaching of evolution, as well as to debates concerning worship or religious symbolism on public property. Some countries in Europe still collect taxes to fund the churches, but even they maintain the separation of religion from government.

Christians have experienced many types of relationships with prevailing governments. Because the Roman Empire first regarded the early church as a branch of Judaism, Christianity was legally protected. But the profession of Christianity soon became a crime, and the degree of persecution or tolerance varied according to the whims of the emperor and the local ruler. Increased martyrdom was accompanied by the flowering of apologetics and theological controversy as well as by the establishment of rank and order in the life of the church. Christians often felt secure from state persecution, but those peaceful times were interspersed with periods of official persecution.

In 303 when Diocletian renewed Roman persecution of Christians, he perceived the church as a political threat, a state within a state, based on the development of an ecclesiastical establishment paralleling his government. Churches were destroyed, clergy imprisoned and forced to sacrifice to Roman gods, sacred books confiscated, and many were martyred. Finally in April 311, an Edict of Toleration of Christians was issued, and in 313 the Emperor Constantine's Edict of Milan gave Christians freedom of conscience. Constantine also transferred his capital from Rome to Byzantium, and the subsequent spread of Christianity more and more coincided with the spread of the Roman Empire.

Constantine, desiring Christianity to be as united as the law and citizenship of the empire, began calling councils of the church to settle theological questions under imperial supervision or control. In May of 325 the first general council was held in Nicea with the bishops attending at government expense. Constantine himself participated and took sides, advocating a specific universal creed. Long after that first council, Christology continued to be debated by theologians and other Christians, and imperial interference continued to play a role. Any departure from official Christian orthodoxy became a state crime.

Subsequent councils were called by the political leaders with the expectation that a united religion would mean a united empire. But just the opposite occurred. Schisms proliferated, and by the close of the sixth century there was profound disaffection from orthodox Christianity, and, therefore, from the government in Constantinople. In parts of the empire, where the churches did not accept the formulation of the 451 Council of Chalcedon, Christians were heavily taxed for disagreeing with the doctrines of the emperor. Abuse and persecution by Byzantine Christians was felt in many parts of the empire. The Persian invasion into parts of Byzantium did nothing to make those same Christians feel less persecuted.

So it was that when the seventh-century Muslim Arab invasion occurred, many Christians welcomed the newcomers as liberators, for the status of Christians under the Islamic protection was often better than under Constantinople or the Persians. Christians, including those affiliated with the empire, were given a special (but secondary) status in society *(dhimmi)*[1] in which they were protected by the government. They were required to pay a tax *(jizya)* in recognition of this submissive status. Laws were enacted imposing social constraints on dress and manners and forbidding the riding and dismounting of animals. The use of religious symbols in public was also forbidden. There were prohibitions against the building of new churches or the repair of existing

---

1. For further explanation of *dhimmi* status, see the boxed text on p. 54.

religious buildings, and Christians were forced to refrain from bell ringing and from the public display of crosses. Non-Muslims were prohibited from missionary activity and Muslims were prohibited from converting to Christianity.

As one model of co-existence, this two-tiered status system, even though it caused some to be second-class citizens, allowed different religious groups to live side by side better than in other parts of the world. The system also, however, reinforced the divisions among churches as it privatized Christianity. As time went on, more and more Christians felt it was better to embrace the new religion than to remain in a subordinate status. Still, Christians thrived in many places; they remained the majority in the region until well into the ninth century.

During these same years, Eastern and Western Christianity became increasingly estranged, both religiously and politically. Western Latin Christianity was much more adversarial toward Islam. The result was the Crusades of the eleventh to thirteenth centuries that began as a desire to free the Holy Land from the Muslims and extended to the sacking of Constantinople and its Eastern churches. This included not only the oppression of the Christian East at the hands of Western Christians but also the oppression of Muslims by Christian nations. Since Islam does not recognize a division between religion and state, it is not surprising that many Muslims fail to see a difference between local Christians and the hostile Western "Christian" governments that were involved in the Crusades.

Several Muslim dynasties followed the Crusades. The last of these was the Ottoman Empire, which established its capital in Constantinople (now Istanbul) in 1453. The Ottomans reinforced the subordinate status of Christians and Jews through the *millet* system, but they also realigned the groups. All Christians who rejected the formulations of the Council of Chalcedon were considered "Armenian" in the eyes of the Ottoman caliph. He also expected the Patriarch of Constantinople to represent all other Christians before his government. The Armenian and Eastern Orthodox patriarchs were expected to control aspects of personal legal life as well as religious regulations for the various churches grouped together. This led to troublesome internal quarrels in the two *millets* as well as to bribery of government officials by several patriarchs.[2]

---

2. For further explanation of the *millet* system, see the boxed text on p. 54.

Late in the Ottoman period, European powers began commercial relationships in the Middle East. They asked for the right to protect individual trading clients (often Christians), and this led to responsibility for whole communities of Christians. Different governments "protected" different churches, which frequently tied Middle Eastern churches to European political centers and feuds. One result was the gradual disruption of the *millet* system, especially as the European governments pressed for equality of citizenship for Christians.

In Islam, religion and state are intertwined in the service of God, and the same person frequently provides both religious and civic leadership. The theological ideal is of a worldwide Muslim community or *'ummah,* in which politics and religion are one and in which racial and ethnic distinctions are unimportant. The religious books of Islam provide the foundation for the legal system, and no Islamic institution parallel to the church was formed. From the beginning, Christian religious leaders had difficulty persuading their Muslim rulers of their civic loyalty since they also wanted to be in contact with the "foreign" religious hierarchy. The protection by European governments raised doubts even further about the civic loyalty of Eastern Christians.

After the defeat of the Ottoman Empire in World War I, the European powers assumed "mandates" in some parts of the empire with the goal of forming nation-states in which citizenship would be based on an individual's place of residence (or birth) rather than on religion, and in which religious organizations would be free from government control. This was in contrast to the concept of *'ummah,* the united community under a single governance with the economic, social, and legal practices based on religion. These two views still vie for acceptance today, and there is as much diversity among the governments of the Middle East concerning the relationship of religion and state as there is in the West.

The following brief reports, on a country-by-country basis, provide a picture of the context in which Christians in the Middle East live today.

Cyprus

Cyprus is located at the crossroads between three continents — Europe, Asia, and Africa. Because of this strategic location, the island has long played a significant role in the Eastern Mediterranean region. Its sunny climate, magnificent scenery, rich history, and pleasant beaches have made Cyprus a favorite among tourists. Because of its general accessibility, Cyprus is a frequent meeting place; it is no accident that seven of the nine general assemblies of the Middle East Council of Churches have been held on the island.

Christian Communities

The Eastern Orthodox family of churches, represented by the autocephalous Church of Cyprus, is by far the largest Christian community here. The Oriental Orthodox family is represented by several Armenian Orthodox congregations.

Within the Catholic family are Maronites, Latin-rite Catholics (most of whom are expatriates), Armenian Catholics, and Melkites.

In the Protestant (Evangelical) family, there is a small Armenian Evangelical community and several Anglican congregations, most of whose members are expatriates. In addition to the above churches that relate to each other ecumenically, there are small communities related to the Church of God of Prophecy, the Community Church in Nicosia, the Greek Evangelical Church, the Christian Brethren, and the Seventh-day Adventist Church.

Christian Population

The Republic of Cyprus is the only country in the Middle East where Christians are in the majority, making up an estimated 80 percent of the total population. The Church of Cyprus represents 98 percent of all Christians there.

Historical Background

The distinctive Greek culture has been evident on Cyprus since 1300 B.C. Christianity traces its history to the visit of St. Paul in A.D. 45. Paul's colleague, Barnabas, became the first bishop, and the church grew rapidly. Three bishops attended the Council of Nicea in 325 and the church was recognized as autocephalous (self-governing) at the Council of Ephesus in 431.

During the Crusades, when Cyprus was ruled by the Franks (crusaders) and later by Venitians, a Latin Catholic hierarchy was installed, deposing Byzantine (Orthodox) prelates. The Latin bishops were themselves expelled by the Turks in 1572. The Byzantine influence has been dominant ever since and the Church of Cyprus has touched virtually every aspect of the island's history, culture, and society. For centuries the Church of Cyprus has provided social welfare, justice, and educational services to the people.

Contemporary Circumstances

Since 1977 the island has been divided with the northern 37 percent of the land occupied by Turkey; the so-called "Turkish Republic of North Cyprus" has not been recognized internationally. The division followed a four-year liberation struggle (1956-60) from nearly a century of British colonial rule. Ethnic tensions also had developed when constitutional amendments proposed by Archbishop Makarios (functioning as president of the new nation) were unacceptable to the minority of ethnic Turks. The invasion by Turkish forces in 1974 forced 180,000 Greek Cypriots (nearly a third of the total Greek Cypriot population) to leave their homes and property in the northern part of the country.

Various attempts to resolve the differences have ended in failure, most recently in 2006. Christian churches in the northern part of the island, many with treasures dating to the Byzantine period, have been robbed and desecrated. In recent years a desire on the part of Greek Cypriots to participate in the European Union has led to occasional tensions with Turkey and also to intermittent efforts to create a federation that recognizes the rights of both ethnic groups. In 2002, efforts by UN Secretary General Kofi Annan to find a formula for unification failed and the Greek part of the island was admitted to the European Union. Some progress toward reunification was made after February 2008; in May 2009 the UN Security Council congratulated both sides and urged an increase in negotiations for peace.

Human rights issues include the plight of refugees from the 1974 invasion, the impact of changes in the island's demography following the arrival of tens of thousands of Turkish settlers, the problems of Greek Cypriots in northern enclaves, and the question of missing and disappeared persons. As in other parts of the world where one religious group dominates the history and contemporary culture, members of minority Christian communities sometimes feel discrimination. Cyprus remains, however, a particularly open and free society and provides a safe venue for many region-wide religious meetings and activities.

The issues of Cyprus have been high on the MECC agenda. The council has often called the problems of a divided Cyprus to the attention of its partners abroad and sought to help create a favorable and supportive climate in which a peaceful resolution to the conflict may be found.

Interfaith Activities

The people who live in the northern part of Cyprus — about 18 percent of the total population of the island — are Sunni Muslims. Because of political tensions, there is very little local interaction between them and the Christians in the south. On a regional basis, however, and especially under the auspices of the Middle East Council of Churches, the Christians of Cyprus have been active in a developing dialogue with Muslims. For the most part, Christians of various denominations in the southern part of the island carry on their own ecumenical relations in the context of the MECC.

Egypt

The Arab Republic of Egypt occupies the northeastern corner of Africa, the Sinai Peninsula, and some islands in the Gulf of Suez and the Red Sea. The northern boundary of Egypt is the Mediterranean Sea, where the Nile spills out through a vast delta. The country is the most populous nation of the Arab world (80.3 million and rapidly growing), with nearly 99 percent of the population living in the Nile valley and delta. The vast majority (90 percent) are Sunni Muslim.

Christian Communities

An overwhelming majority of Christians in the country are communicants of the Coptic Orthodox Church; two other Oriental Orthodox churches represented in Egypt are the Armenian Apostolic and the Syriac Orthodox churches.

The Eastern Orthodox family is represented by the Greek Orthodox Patriarchate of Alexandria and All Africa.

The Catholic family is represented in Egypt by the Coptic Catholic Church, as well as by Melkites, Latin-rite Catholics (most of whom are expatriates), Maronites, Syriac Catholics, Armenian Catholics, and Chaldean Catholics.

The Evangelical family is represented by the relatively strong Evangelical Church of Egypt (Synod of the Nile), by an Anglican community (an estimated half of whom are expatriates), and by the Armenian Evangelical Church. In addition, there are small groups related to the

Assemblies of God, Christian Brethren, Free Methodist, the Gospel Preaching Church, Pentecostal, Seventh-day Adventist, Church of God, and the Churches of Christ. The Evangelical churches are represented by the Protestant Community of Egypt, whose organization and functions are rooted in the *millet* system of the Ottoman Empire.[1]

Christian Population

Christians constitute an estimated 10 percent of Egypt's population. Approximately 95 percent of the Christians in Egypt are related to the Coptic Orthodox Church, the largest Christian community in the Middle East. The next largest group of Christians in Egypt is the Coptic Catholic Church with an estimated 2.5 percent.

Historical Background

Egypt has one of the oldest and best-preserved civilizations in the world. First united into a single state five thousand years ago, it was a great power for much of the next three thousand years. Its influence decreased when it became a province of the Roman Empire thirty years before Christ. It was not until the Arabs drove out the Byzantine forces in the seventh century A.D. that Egypt began to reclaim a central role in the Middle East.

During the centuries between the birth of Christ and the arrival of the Arabs, Egypt was a Christian country in which theology and education flourished. Two Egyptian churches, the Greek Orthodox Patriarchate of Alexandria and the Coptic Orthodox Church, both trace their roots to apostolic times. Claiming the authority of the early Christian historian, Eusebius, the Copts trace the origins of Egyptian Christianity to the martyrdom of St. Mark in Alexandria. When the church split in 451 over the theological formulations of the Council of Chalcedon, the majority became the Coptic Orthodox Church. The modern cathedral in Cairo, named for the apostle, now

---

1. For further explanation of the *millet* system, see "A Brief History" at the beginning of this chapter and the boxed text on p. 54.

St. Catherine's Monastery

To visit this site you begin by getting up very, very early. By perseverance, climbing, perhaps riding a camel partway, more climbing, and cups of hot tea at little kiosks, you make it to the top of Mount Sinai (or Mt. Moses) by dawn. As you gasp for breath, you wonder that Moses could make several round-trips up and down. This is the best-known possible site for Mt. Horeb in the Sinai Penninsula, where Moses received the tablets of the Law. After your descent, the Monastery of St. Catherine beckons and you are surprised by the best part of the trip.

Christian pilgrims came to the area of the Burning Bush by the third century, and monks arrived in the fourth century to form communities or to live as hermits (anchorites). As protection for the monks, Emperor Justinian fortified a monastery in 528, incorporating the fourth-century Chapel of the Burning Bush. Although nomadic tribes often attacked the monastery, parts of it have survived from the early years. Since 528 it has come under the protection of successive conquering governments.

The original wooden doors are intact along with ancient mosaics, crusader carvings, and a seventeenth-century iconostasis covered with gold. A famous gallery contains two thousand icons, including some of the few sixth-century icons to survive the Iconoclastic Controversy, when most icons were destroyed throughout the Byzantine Empire. Priceless manuscripts and books are contained in the library and the skulls of dead monks are still visible in the Charnel House. The greatest threat today is the influx of tourists that disturbs the monastic atmosphere.

shelters relics of the saint that were returned from Venice in 1968 by Pope Paul VI.

After the Arab invasion in 642, Christians were persecuted and many converted to Islam. In modern times, Napoleon invaded Egypt in 1798, and, although he withdrew three years later, the nation had been opened to Western influences. After the British invaded in 1882, the

Copts played important roles in the management of business and the administration of the state until Colonel Gamal Abdul Nasser became President in 1952.

The Copts are probably the least-mixed descendants of Egypt's pre-Arab population; the word "Coptic" simply means Egyptian, though today it designates any Egyptian Christian.

Contemporary Circumstances

A number of religion-based groups, particularly the Islamic political movement, play an increasingly important role in Egypt's social and political life. In the 1970s, responding to pressure from this movement, President Anwar Sadat placed Pope Shenouda III and several Coptic Orthodox clergy under house arrest in the Wadi Natroun monasteries. Following his release by President Mubarak, Pope Shenouda has led a revival in his church, with a major emphasis on education, youth activities, and the church's ancient monastic tradition.

The churches function with government permission and generally quite openly. The building and repair of Christian religious buildings is restricted, requiring provincial governor approval; nevertheless, because Christians, especially the Copts, have a high level of education and are active in cultural, social, and economic organizations, they have been disproportionately represented in civil service positions. Christians generally were disappointed by recent legal reforms but remain supportive of their government and the Egyptian national cause.

The Muslim Brotherhood is perhaps the largest and best-organized of the aforementioned political/religious groups; its major goal is the implementation of Islamic *shar'ia* law in all social, political, and legislative aspects of life. Some of the religion-based groups prefer violence and terrorism to political influence and call for the establishment of an Islamic state. The government has restricted their efforts but they remain active, especially in towns and villages in Upper Egypt.

Extremists occasionally have torched Christian churches in a challenge to the government's policy guaranteeing security for both citizens and visitors. In one incident in the Minya district of Upper Egypt, nine Coptic Orthodox young people were killed and seven others

Wadi Natroun

About sixty-five miles from the over-crowded, noisy, dusty streets of Cairo you can enter the world of fourth-century Christianity in the monasteries of Wadi Natroun. The monastic movement is based on the idea of abstaining from temporary pleasures as a sacrifice for God's sake. St. Anthony and his followers lived as hermits for periods of time but also opened their caves to philosophers and theologians. Another form of monasticism includes the communal orders established at Wadi Natroun by St. Macarius, a combination of hermit life during the week and communal life on Sundays. Coptic asceticism has had a profound effect on the whole Coptic Church in that religious practice for ordinary people includes fast days for more than half of the year.

Egyptian monasteries for men and women are experiencing a revival today with greater numbers of monks as well as renovations and rebuilding, especially after Pope Shenouda III was put under house arrest in Wadi Natroun. Following Pope Shenouda's forced isolation, the monasteries (for men and women) in Egypt have held conferences and events for youth; families go to spend weekends among the monks, seeking wisdom, spiritual advice, and a respite from city life. Few of the monks today are hermits but most live in a communal system.

There are four monasteries (out of fifty) left in Wadi Natroun: Deir Abu Maqar (St. Macarius), Deir Anba Bishoi, Deir el Suriani, and Deir el Baramous. Icons, carved doors, chapels, and churches are available for viewing as well as the "keep," an area designed to keep monks safe from marauders. Often only one or two of the monasteries are open to the public at the same time.

wounded when five fanatics burst into a church and opened fire. Islamic leaders were quick to denounce the killings and the Muslim Brotherhood eventually joined in unambiguous condemnation. The small group that claimed responsibility seemed to be pressing the Brotherhood to more aggressive action at a time when interreligious dialogue and cooperation were increasing. Occasional attacks on Christians or their churches, while regarded as isolated events, receive immediate government attention. That was the case in January 2010 after an attack at an ancient Coptic site in Nag Hammadi.

Interfaith Activities

The Middle East Council of Churches (which maintains an office in Cairo and conducts a variety of programs in Egypt) and the Coptic Orthodox Church are seeking to build bridges of understanding and reconciliation as they pursue the goal of a just and stable society for all Egyptians. In 1997 Pope Shenouda rejected as interference a proposed U.S. congressional effort to monitor and punish Christian persecution in Egypt, saying, "Whatever problems the Copts of Egypt are suffering will be solved within a domestic framework and through purely Egyptian channels." Following the 2010 attack in Nag Hammadi, in which six persons were killed and others were injured, the World Council of Churches expressed deep concern, but encouraged Pope Shenouda and other Christian leaders to "continue to counter negative trends with pro-active engagement in dialogue and partnership for life and for Christian-Muslim coexistence."

The Holy Land: Israel and Palestine

For several reasons, the Holy Land is unique. Bethlehem was where Jesus was born; Jerusalem the city of his trial, his death, and his resurrection. Jerusalem also was the city in which, at Pentecost, the church was born, and from which it spread around the globe. For nearly two thousand years there has been a worshiping Christian community in the Holy Land. Perhaps nowhere in the world are so many parts of the Christian Church represented — even though some are very small expatriate groups. Palestine and Israel are also, however, home to two other world religions: Judaism and Islam. Today in the Holy Land, Christianity is a "double minority," existing with varying degrees of discomfort alongside two much larger religious communities.

Christian pilgrims visit the Holy Land, eager to walk in the footsteps of Christ, to see the places about which they have studied, and to encounter the "living stones" — those women and men who find their hometowns when they open Scripture. Israel and Palestine are not only central to the biblical faith; they are at the center of the world's attention as two peoples (Israelis and Palestinians) and three faiths struggle to discover the necessary elements of a just peace. Despite the fact that Israel and Palestine are discrete entities, separated from each other by a high wall and barbed wire, difficult checkpoints, and deep emotions, nearly all of the traditional and nonconciliar churches function in both areas with single, unified ecclesiastical structures. For that reason, the churches of Israel and Palestine are treated together in the paragraphs that follow.

Church of the Annunciation

As you wind your way down from the hills into the bowl that is the city of Nazareth, Israel, the most impressive sight is the tower of the Church of the Annunciation, built like a lantern atop one of the largest churches in the Middle East. This Latin (Roman) Catholic Church was built over the ruins of an early Jewish-Christian synagogue, a fifth-century basilica, a crusader church, and a modest Franciscan church dating from 1730. Other denominations have churches in Nazareth honoring people and events in Jesus' life and hometown, but this church is the landmark.

The 1969 church is an upper level, with an octagonal rotunda looking down through the floor onto the grotto of the annunciation and a U-shaped area used for celebrating the Eucharist, especially by visiting tour groups. There are massive bronze doors as well as outstanding façades and chapels, but the greatest attraction is the series of frescoes and mosaics from around the world depicting Mary, often with Jesus. The style of the art and the people depicted are representative of the country from which the piece was sent.

As the city of Nazareth was preparing for the A.D. 2000 celebration, a controversy arose because Israeli officials had given permission for Muslims to build a mosque with a high minaret immediately in front of the church on property that had been planned for a park. The controversy was settled by placing the new mosque in a different part of the city but it had negative effects on Christian/Muslim relations in this largely Christian city.

Christian Communities

The Eastern Orthodox family of churches is represented in the Holy Land by relatively strong parishes of the Greek Orthodox Patriarchate of Jerusalem, by small Russian communities related to the Moscow Patriarchate which now includes the Russian Orthodox Church Outside Russia, and by a small Romanian community with ties to the Orthodox Church of Romania.

The Oriental Orthodox family is represented by the Jerusalem Patriarchate of the Armenian Apostolic Church (related to the Catholicos of All Armenians in Etchmiadzin, Armenia) and by Coptic Orthodox, Ethiopian Orthodox, and Syriac Orthodox communities. The last three are related to patriarchates in Cairo, Addis Ababa, and Damascus, respectively. Each of the groups is relatively small and generally made up of individuals or families who originally came to the area for religious reasons, or, in the case of the Armenians, to escape religious and ethnic persecution.

The Catholic family includes parishes related to the Latin Patriarchate of Jerusalem; the Patriarchal Exarchates of the Greek Catholic, Maronite, Syriac Catholic, and Armenian Catholic churches; and the Chaldean Patriarchal Vicariate.

The Evangelical family includes parishes of the Episcopal Church in Jerusalem and the Middle East and the Evangelical Lutheran Church in Jordan and the Holy Land. There also are Lutheran missions or congregations related to Lutheran bodies in Denmark, Finland, Germany, Norway, Sweden, and the United States. In addition, there are two congregations related to the Church of Scotland (Presbyterian).

There also are congregations related to Baptist bodies, the Christian and Missionary Alliance, Christian Brethren, Church of God, Church of the Nazarene, French Protestants, King of Kings Assembly, Korean Presbyterians, Netherland Reformed, Pentecostal, and Seventh-day Adventists, as well as interdenominational congregations. In addition there are several groups of Messianic Jews who acknowledge Yeshua (Jesus) as the Messiah but who follow some Jewish practices.

Christian Population

The most significant demographic change in the entire region during the twentieth century took place in Israel and occupied East Jerusalem. The Israeli basic law affirms the right of any Jew, anyplace in the world, to move to Israel. Nearly five million have done so — often because they felt unwelcome elsewhere. In the process, however, the indigenous Arab population, both Muslims and Christians, have either left or experienced religious, economic, and political stress.

Within the 1948 borders of the State of Israel, there are today about 105,000 Christians, approximately 2 percent of the total population.

(There are an estimated 720,000 Muslims and 82,000 Druzes.) The Christians live mainly in or near the Galilee cities of Haifa and Nazareth, with smaller numbers in the ancient port city of Jaffa and nearby in Ramle and Lydda (Lod). The largest Christian communities in Israel are Greek Catholics (Melkites) and Greek Orthodox, with Latin-rite and Maronite Catholics third and fourth. There are much smaller numbers of Armenians, Anglicans, and Lutherans, and relatively few representatives of the other churches.

In Palestine (including Gaza, the West Bank, and occupied East Jerusalem) there are an estimated 76,000 Christians who represent 3 percent of the total population. More than half of these Christians belong to Greek Orthodox parishes. Latin-rite Catholics number about 15,000, with Melkites approximately 4,000. Armenians, Copts, Syriac Orthodox, Anglicans, and Lutherans each count around 2,500. Very small numbers of other ethnic Christians make up the balance. Within the Latin-rite Catholic community there are significant numbers of Franciscans (who have been assigned "custody" of certain holy places), as well as members of other orders who come from overseas. In Gaza, where Christianity dates to the preaching of the Apostle Philip and where St. Hilarion established the world's first monastery in 290, there are today only about 2,000 Christians. Most of these are well educated, working in such professions and medicine and engineering.

Historical Background

The maps of Israel and Palestine are dotted with settlements and villages, towns and cities right out of the Bible. Each of the three religions has sacred places and buildings that mark their histories. Sometimes, where those histories coincide or overlap, the holy places are shared or, more often, contested. The historical background, then, begins with the long history of the three faiths. From Pentecost to A.D. 70 Palestine was a Roman province populated largely by Jews. The destruction of Jerusalem in that year by Emperor Titus was followed by revolts that led the Romans to forbid Jews from entering after Hadrian rebuilt the city in 135. Five hundred years later, in 614, Persians conquered the Holy Land and destroyed all its many Christian churches except for the Church of the Nativity in Bethlehem (spared because of its connection

Church of the Holy Sepulchre

In the middle of the Old City of Jerusalem stands what some consider the holiest church of the Christian world and others consider an overrated tourist site. It is in the early morning when the local Christians stop on their way to work that it seems to function as a church. Even earlier in the morning the ritual of opening takes place with representatives of two Muslim families who by long tradition have control of the key unlocking the door. Three bells verify for the Catholics, Armenians, and Greek Orthodox that the church (called the Church of the Resurrection by the Eastern Orthodox) is officially opened.

The earliest shrine on the site marked the place of Jesus' crucifixion and the tomb in which his body was laid. A pagan temple was built by Emperor Hadrian in 135 to discourage Christian veneration of the holy site, and its history includes buildings by Constantine I and the crusaders as well as the destruction by the Persians, by Caliph Hakim the Mad, and by fire and earthquakes. In 638 the Muslim Caliph Omar guaranteed the church to the Christians by refusing to pray inside, and in 1852 the Status Quo determined the times and places where specified denominations may hold services and even clean the pavement.

The dome was damaged in an earthquake in 1927, and repaired but not decorated due to the lack of agreement among the Armenians, Catholics, and Greek Orthodox. In 1997 a new dome was dedicated by all three patriarchs. Its abstract design of white and gold around a sixteen-foot skylight suggests a sunburst.

to the Magi). Muslim Arabs, who gained control in 636, were driven out in 1099 by the crusaders. The crusaders built many churches and fortresses before they were themselves defeated in 1187 by Saladin.

From 1517 until 1917 the Holy Land was under the control of the Ottoman Turks, who supported Germany in World War I. Following that war, the British mandate from the League of Nations led to a volatile period triggered in part by the Balfour Declaration, which viewed "with favor the establishment in Palestine of a home for the Jewish people." Jews, including many fleeing Nazi Germany, began to arrive and the British were unable to cope with the mounting conflict between Zionist terror groups and the indigenous Arab population. Following World War II, the British turned the question over to the United Nations, which adopted a partition plan in November 1947, giving 54 percent of Palestine to the Jews, who at that time made up one-third of the population and owned less than 10 percent of the land. The Arabs rejected this partition. The British withdrew in May 1948, and the State of Israel was proclaimed, leading to the first of several wars.

As a result of what the Israelis call the War of Independence and Palestinians call *Al-Naqba,* the Catastrophe, 726,000 Christian and Muslim refugees were driven out or fled, seeking haven in neighboring countries, Gaza, and the West Bank. The latter became part of Jordan. In the so-called Six Day War of 1967, Israel captured Gaza and the West Bank, including East Jerusalem, which was annexed. Since then Israel has built settlements on confiscated land throughout the West Bank. Israel also annexed the Golan Heights, captured from Syria. The annexations and settlement-building are in defiance of international law.

A peace process was based on the "Declaration of Principles" signed by Israel and the Palestine Liberation Organization on September 13, 1993. Following Israeli withdrawal from Jericho and parts of the Gaza Strip in 1994, six West Bank cities (including Bethlehem) came under Palestinian control in 1995 as did a major part of Hebron in 1997. But in 2002 Israel reoccupied those cities in a series of incursions designed, it said, to prevent suicide bombing and other attacks. Israel unilaterally withdrew its army and several settlements from Gaza in 2005 but retained control of all access to and from Gaza, effectively sealing off the 139 square mile area from all contact.

This extreme isolation led to shortages of such basic necessities as food, fuel, and medical supplies, and the people of Gaza in 2007 elected members of Hamas to represent them in the Palestinian parliament. Thus controlling the most densely populated area in the world, Hamas permitted occasional rocket attacks on nearby Israeli communities.

Also in 2007, the World Council of Churches held a conference nearby in Jordan. Delegates from many nations issued what became known as the Amman Call. It urged Israel and the Palestinians to achieve a two-state solution, ensuring security for Israel. The call acknowledged that Israeli settlements in the occupied territories are "illegal and an obstacle to peace" and insisted that the wall then being constructed by Israel "must be removed from Palestinian territory." As part of the Amman Call, the WCC organized a Palestine Israel Ecumenical Forum to encourage new and existing church efforts for peace in the region.

After harsh Israeli responses to sporadic rocket attacks from Gaza, by mid-2009 Hamas unilaterally declared a temporary truce. As the truce was about to expire, Israel sent tanks across the border and dropped bombs that hit residential areas, schools, hospitals, and even United Nations installations. Israel claimed militants were harbored in the targeted areas. Thousands of homes were destroyed, along with such basic infrastructure as water and power supplies. Israel was severely criticized throughout the world for "Operation Cast Lead," which began after Christmas 2008 and lasted into 2009.

Against that background, a group of church leaders and representatives from Palestinian civil society and international organizations met in Bethlehem and issued a theological statement known as the Kairos Palestine Document. The initiative was launched at a ceremony in December 2009 at the International Center of Christmas Evangelical Lutheran Church in Bethlehem. Among the participants were representatives of the Latin and Greek Orthodox Patriarchates, the Sabeel Liberation Theology movement, *Al Liqa,* the World Council of Churches, and several of its member churches.

Contemporary Circumstances

More than in most other parts of the Middle East, the Christian community in the Holy Land clearly is endangered. The flight of refugees in 1948 and 1967 has been matched by recurring waves of emigration. A desperate economic situation, especially following the "closure" of the borders between the Palestinian territories and Jerusalem or Israel proper, has led many Christians to seek improved circumstances for themselves and their children. There have been other factors, as well. Land confiscation, severe travel restrictions, the impact of settlement-building on the character of Jerusalem, an arbitrary system of permits, the confiscation of identification cards, the construction of a 25-foot-

Church of the Nativity

The Church of the Nativity in Bethlehem, occupied West Bank, is considered to be the oldest Christian church in continuous use anywhere in the world. It was built in the sixth century over the ruins of a fourth-century church. Tradition says that the earliest church on the site was built over the cave where Jesus was born. Today's church incorporates a grotto that is believed to be from the oldest church. The church survived because the Persians, who conquered the Holy Land in 614, noticed that the frescoes contained pictures of the Wise Men thought to have come from ancient Persia. In deference to their own country, they left this church intact while destroying all other churches in the Holy Land.

The present complex includes the Latin Catholic Church of St. Catherine of Alexandria as well as three monasteries that serve Latin Catholics, Greek Orthodox, and Armenian Orthodox. The Church of the Nativity is entered through a low door called the "Door of Humility," reputed to have been constructed so pilgrims would bow down. In fact, the lintel was lowered to prevent horses and carriages from entering. The church has a simple interior with traces of early frescoes and mosaic floors. This is one of the holy sites covered by the 1852 Status Quo document that regulates times and areas of use of holy sites by various denominations.

The use of the church as a place of sanctuary in 2002 is a reminder that one of the traditional functions of religious places (churches, mosques, and synagogues) is as a haven of safety. Palestinians also fled to the church in 1967 during the Israeli occupation — as others probably did many other times in history.

high wall that isolates Palestinian communities, harsh occupation — all these have contributed to hopelessness and despair. At least 250,000 Palestinian Christians live in the diaspora, more than 60 percent of all Palestinian Christians worldwide.

As increasing numbers have joined family and friends in Europe, the Americas, and Australia, cities that once had Christian majorities have become Jewish or Muslim. In Jerusalem, for example, there were 31,000 Palestinian Christians in 1947; today there are fewer than 10,000. Afif Safieh, Palestinian ambassador to the United Kingdom and the Holy See at the time, reported to the World Council of Churches that "you have many more Christian Palestinians in Chile than you have in Palestine; you have many more Christians *from* Jerusalem living in Sydney, Australia, than you have Christians *in* Jerusalem."

Christian communities in the northern part of the West Bank have been cut off from those in the southern part and their members generally are prevented by Israel from reaching the holy places in Jerusalem. Within Israel proper, Christians in places like Nazareth live as second- or third-class citizens. Arabs who live in Israel — whether Christian or Muslim — normally are unable to serve in the armed forces, and many educational and social services are based on military service. In 2009 Israel began deleting Arabic designations of Muslim and Christian sites, some with biblical names, from street signs in Jerusalem and Israel, using only Hebrew names. According to the chief justice of Palestine, who resides in occupied East Jerusalem, "This is the implementation of the Israeli strategy aimed at the abolition of Arab identity that obliterates heritage and culture and uproots Palestinians from their homeland. It is part of the campaign to Judaize the holy city." Some persons believe that the Christian heritage also will be obliterated.

Israeli media have reported that Christians are experiencing repression and persecution from their Muslim neighbors and the Palestinian Authority. These charges have been denied by the leaders of the historic churches who point out that immediately after the Israeli occupation forces left Bethlehem, the Palestinian Authority's president Yasser Arafat proclaimed Christmas a national holiday in Palestine. Six of the eighty-six seats on the Legislative Council are designated for Christians. Both Muslims and Christians in the Holy Land are quick to identify themselves and each other as Palestinians.

Both the Israeli government and the Palestinian Authority maintain offices for religious affairs. It is through these offices that church officials have formal contact with the governments.

Interfaith Activities

The Christian leaders in the Holy Land are involved in multiple approaches to dialogue and work with their Jewish and Muslim counterparts. In addition to the region-wide activities developed through the Middle East Council of Churches several local efforts have been undertaken despite the tensions and problems that exist. Scholarly work involving lay and clergy representatives of all three faith groups has been initiated under the auspices of a Bethlehem-based organization known as *Al-Liqa,* an Arabic word that translates "Encounter." Conferences, roundtable discussions, research, and a journal have characterized the efforts. The Interreligious Coordinating Council in Israel provides a focus for Jewish-Christian and Jewish-Muslim discussions and so-called "trialogues," and seeks to draw together representatives of various organizations of the three faith groups. The ICCI has also sponsored speaking tours for representatives of the three groups in the United States and elsewhere. The Interfaith Encounter Association, based in Jerusalem, includes a women's encounter section that has held events for Christian, Muslim, Jewish, Druze, and Baha'i women. A group known as Beit Hegeffen, in Haifa, has sought to bring together clergy of the three faith groups. The patriarchs and heads of the historic Christian churches have reached out to Muslim and Jewish counterparts in an effort to seek a common ground for a just peace. Islamic leaders in Jerusalem have long welcomed that initiative and recently the Chief Rabbis have participated in a new Council of Religious Institutions.

Iran

In ancient times, Persia was a powerful force, stretching from the Eastern Mediterranean to Central Asia and often at odds with the countries to its West. In 1971, Iran (modern-day Persia) celebrated 2,500 years of rule by monarchy. Eight years later, the Shah was deposed and the Islamic Republic of Iran proclaimed. Iran is today the world's major stronghold of Shi'ite Islam. The country has a population of more than seventy million, 22 percent of whom are under the age of fourteen.

Christian Communities

The Eastern Orthodox family is represented in Iran by relatively small communities related to the Greek Orthodox Church of Antioch and to the Russian Orthodox Church.

The Oriental Orthodox family is represented by congregations of the Armenian Apostolic Church, many of whose members are descendants of persons who fled there at the time of the genocide. Armenians represent the largest Christian group.

The Catholic family includes parishes related to the Chaldean Catholic Church, the Armenian Catholic Church, and Latin-rite Catholics (mostly expatriates).

The Evangelical family includes the Evangelical Church in Iran (Presbyterian) and several Anglican parishes (half of whose members are expatriates). Unaffiliated Protestant bodies include congregations of the Assemblies of God and several other small groups of believers.

In addition, there are congregations associated with the Assyrian Church of the East, an ancient church that now has its patriarchal see in the United States. It is not in communion with any other religious body and is not part of any of the four families of churches.

Christian Population

Christians in Iran make up less than 1 percent of the total population. The largest group of Christians, estimated at more than 200,000 believers in some thirty-five parishes, are Armenian Orthodox whose ties are to the Catholicosate of Cilicia (in Lebanon). The Armenian Orthodox are part of an identifiable ethnic group and, as is the case with the Assyrian and Chaldean Catholic communities in Iran, their services are carried out in their own languages. The numbers of Anglicans and Presbyterians (known locally as Evangelicals) were very small even before the Islamic revolution of 1979. More than half of the Anglicans and Presbyterians are expatriates.

Historical Background

Apostolic Christianity did not take root in the Iranian kingdom as it did in some other countries (such as Armenia, Syria, and Egypt) largely because of the strength of the Zoroastrian religion. The Assyrian Church of the East did enjoy a significant period of growth and missionary activity during which the church spread through Central Asia to China. Eventually, however, in Persia as well as farther east, the church lost strength with the advance of Muslim and Mongol forces. Today approximately 89 percent of the country's population are Shi'ites with Sunnis making up another 9 percent. The largest minority are the Baha'i. In addition to the Christians there are also a few Jews and some Zoroastrians.

Franciscan and Dominican priests arrived at the end of the thirteenth century, but their efforts ended within one hundred years because of a plague and the invasion of Tamerlane. New Latin Catholic efforts began in the seventeenth century and after World War II but these served mainly expatriates. The Armenian Christian enclave developed in the seventeenth century, when Armenians were employed to help build the city of New Julfa. Anglican missionaries from England arrived in 1832 and Presbyterians came from the United States in 1855, opening schools and hospitals as well as churches.

Contemporary Circumstances

About 90 percent of Iran's Christians, notably the Armenians and Chaldeans, practice their religion without hindrance. As recently as 1982, the government issued a Christmas stamp with the inscription, "Glorification of Christ's Birth." On the other hand, most of the ten to fifteen thousand Protestants worship in the national language, Farsi, and disseminate Bibles and literature in that language. They accept and even seek converts from Islam, which has led to institutionalized discrimination and persecution against them. The Protestants' ties to the West, as well as the hospitality shown to them earlier by the Shah, have made them suspect. In 1990, an Evangelical pastor, himself a convert from Islam, was charged with apostasy, sentenced to death, and executed.

Human Rights Watch has documented a number of cases and points out that although Orthodox minorities have suffered less and are able to practice their faith more openly, they are subject to some discrimination as well. The Christian religious authorities administer personal status courts for marriages, divorce, and inheritance. According to Human Rights Watch, however, in lower levels of the public courts, where the *shar'ia* law is the basis for the legal code, judges "take decisions that very often favor the Muslims."[1] As in other Middle Eastern countries, the Christian population is declining, partly by emigration. It is estimated that nearly 20,000 Christians leave their country every year.

Interfaith Activities

The Middle East Council of Churches has participated in an ongoing dialogue in Iran, organized jointly by the World Council of Churches and the Organization of Islamic Culture and Communication. In 1996

1. "Iran: Religious and Ethnic Minorities: Discrimination in Law and Practice," *Human Rights Watch Report*, vol. 9, no. 7 (Sept. 1997). This report and others can be found at www.hrw.org.

the conference agreed to explore ways in which Muslims and Christians can collaborate on human rights issues. The government that was elected in 1998 appears open to dialogue. At the grassroots level, however, interfaith encounters are rare.

Iraq

Once known as Mesopotamia — the "land between the rivers" — the Republic of Iraq was the site of ancient Babylon and Assyria. The valleys and tributaries of the Tigris and Euphrates rivers were the cradle of one of the earliest civilizations. One of the seven wonders of the ancient world was Babylon's hanging gardens; as significant were Hammurabi's first-known code of laws and the development of cuneiform writing. Modern Iraq is home to 27.5 million people, 80 percent of whom are Arabs. About half of the population are Shi'ite Muslims, nearly all of whom live in the south. The Sunni are about equally divided between scattered Arab communities and the Kurds, who live in the north. The Kurdish desire for self-government has been the source of long-standing conflicts and at least one massacre, during the authoritarian and ruthless rule of President Saddam Hussein. In the violent instability that has followed the U.S.-led invasion in 2003 the ethnic Kurds have been among the targets of insurgent bombers and various forms of intimidation and political pressure. UN refugee agencies estimated that more than two million Iraqis have fled their country; of these between 250,000 and 500,000 are estimated to be Christians.

Christian Communities

The Eastern Orthodox family of churches is represented in Iraq by communicants of the Greek Orthodox Church of Antioch.

Three Oriental Orthodox communities have parishes in Iraq: the

Syriac Orthodox Church, the Armenian Apostolic Church, and the Coptic Orthodox Church.

The Catholic family of churches includes parishes related to the Chaldean Catholic Church, the Armenian Catholic Church, the Greek Catholic (Melkite) Church, and expatriates associated with Latin-rite congregations.

The Evangelical family is represented by members of five isolated Reformed and Anglican parishes. These congregations historically were related to churches in the Persian Gulf (see p. 189). There is also a small Seventh-day Adventist community and several other small unaffiliated Protestant bodies.

In addition, there are congregations associated with the Assyrian Church of the East, an ancient church that now has its patriarchal see in the United States. It is not in communion with any other religious body and is not part of any of the four families of churches.

Christian Population

There were nearly a million Christians in Iraq, or roughly 3 percent of the population, before the U.S. invasion in 2003. By far the largest Christian group was the Chaldean Catholics, who made up more than two-thirds of all the Christians. Of the other Catholic communities, the Syriac Catholic Church had the most significant numbers; the Armenian, Latin, and Greek (Melkite) Catholics were relatively small. Both the Chaldean Catholic Church and Assyrian Church of the East originated in the area and were more numerous in Iraq than in other Middle Eastern countries. The Assyrians, strongest in Kurdish areas of the north, suffered great losses from massacres at the hands of Ottoman Turks in the second half of the nineteenth century and in 1933 by Iraqis following independence. That led to major emigrations to the United States, where the Assyrian community is larger than in Iraq. The other Christian communities also have been diminished by emigration, especially after 2003. The Syriac Orthodox and the Armenian Apostolic churches are the only others with memberships greater than ten thousand. All Christian groups have dramatically lost numbers as refugees fled to Syria, Jordan, and Lebanon. Bernard Sabella, a prominent Christian sociologist in Palestine, has estimated that "there are probably more Assyrian [Christians] in the Swedish city of Sodertalje than in the province of Ninawa and northern Iraq combined."

Historical Background

The seventh century saw the Islamic conquest of Iraq, which was ruled by the Umayyads from Syria. When the Abbasid dynasty came to power a century later it ruled its enormous empire from Baghdad. Later, having lost its importance following the Mongol destruction of Baghdad in 1258, Iraq was part of the Ottoman Empire from the sixteenth to the early twentieth centuries.

Iraq became independent in 1932, following more than a decade of control by the British under a League of Nations mandate. That year a monarchy with close ties to Great Britain was established under King Faisal I. The first of a series of coups took place in 1958 and a republic was created. By 1968 Saddam Hussein was playing a decisive role, and he became president in 1979, representing one wing of the secular and pan-Arab philosophy of the Ba'ath Party. During a long (1980-88) war between Iraq and Iran, the U.S.A. supported Iraq.

The Gulf War of 1991 followed an Iraqi effort to dominate Kuwait and its rich oil deposits. The aftermath of that war, including a severe embargo on Iraq imposed by the United Nations, sharply divided the Arab world and created circumstances of great human need within Iraq. As a result of the 2003 invasion, Saddam Hussein was overthrown and a new government was elected. Hussein was captured in December 2003, tried, and finally executed in December 2006. Although the elected government includes representatives of all major religious groups, bitter divisions between Sunni and Shia Muslims have made governance very difficult. The fragile government has had trouble maintaining order and a stable economy. U.S. and other coalition forces have announced their intention to leave Iraq in 2011.

Contemporary Circumstances

The Christian minority who are left in Iraq live in ambivalent and difficult circumstances. The political situation tends to limit the role of religious groups, asserting that a common Arab identity is required as the base for the Iraqi state. Islam is recognized as a state religion, though freedom of worship for all citizens is constitutionally affirmed. Christians, however, have been harassed in part because their loyalties have been questioned. Militant Muslim groups have assumed that Iraqi Christians have aided the U.S. and its coalition partners, who are considered the "Christian West." Observant Muslims have sometimes violently forced stores selling alcoholic beverages to close. Many Christians have been attacked because of their relative economic wealth: some have been forced to pay "protection fees" or, if they emigrate to pay the militants excessive "departure taxes" of $200 per person and $400 per car. These departures often have been sudden, with the refugees leaving everything behind.

In the Baghdad suburb of Dora, the largest Christian enclave, only families agreeing to give a daughter or sister in marriage to a Muslim were permitted to remain. This was also the site in June and July of 2009 of several church bombings.

Nevertheless, both Catholic and Protestant church leaders in Iraq have urged Christians to stay or return to their homes. "Christians can play an important role in rebuilding Iraq," a Chaldean Catholic bishop told a meeting sponsored by the World Council of Churches in 2009. In the face of critical humanitarian needs, Iraqi churches have sought to cooperate with the UN, the Red Cross and Red Crescent Societies, and have been the conduits for international Christian assistance frequently facilitated by the Middle East Council of Churches.

Under Sadam Hussein Christians for the most part enjoyed relative economic comfort; many were highly educated and were both professional and educational leaders. With a few prominent exceptions, however, Christians are virtually excluded from public life. In the present situation most Christians avoid political involvement. The lack of socioeconomic stability has prompted religious extremism, including incidents aimed at Christian centers.

Interfaith Activities

Because of their preoccupation with the humanitarian crisis that developed as a result of years of fighting and the general lack of security,

Iraqi Christians have not been engaged in local dialogue with Muslims. Some leaders who travel outside the country have participated in conversations initiated by ecumenical bodies, including the World Council of Churches and the Middle East Council of Churches.

Jordan

The modern Hashemite Kingdom of Jordan was created following World War I when Great Britain received a League of Nations mandate for the region of Palestine. Transjordan, established as a separate mandatory state, gained independence in 1946 and became the Hashemite Kingdom in 1950. Today Jordan continues to enjoy strong economic and personal ties to both England and the United States. Jordan's relation to the Holy Land is both historic and strategic. In biblical times, Jordan was home to Amorites, Moabites, Edomites, and others. There are references in the Gospels as well. A credible location of Jesus' baptism in the Jordan River is on what is now the Jordanian side, just north of the Dead Sea. Farther north is Pella, one of the cities of the Decapolis visited by Jesus and the disciples and which offered hospitality to fleeing Christians who sought to escape Roman forces in A.D. 66 and 135. Following the Council of Nicea, Pella was an important episcopal see.

During the Arab-Israeli War in 1948, Jordan occupied the West Bank, including East Jerusalem. Its strong interest in the Muslim holy places on the Haram al Sherif became formal during that period. Since 1967, Israel has controlled the West Bank, but having signed a peace treaty with Israel in 1994, Jordan today plays an increasingly significant role in the search for stability and peace throughout the region.

The Madaba Mosaic

The Madaba Mosaic isn't in perfect shape. It isn't all there, and it isn't even based on an accurate map. The original mosaic floor in St. George's Orthodox Church in Madaba, Jordan, was constructed in the sixth century. The map was rediscovered in 1884 and identified as the floor of a great Byzantine cathedral and then incorporated into a new church.

Visitors looking for an unusual church or even a complete map of the area will be disappointed, but a careful viewing shows the humor and sensitivity of the artist. There are fish swimming in the Jordan River both toward and away from the Dead Sea and a gazelle jumping about near a lion. Two enormous boats ply the Dead Sea.

The best known, and probably most important, part of the map is the detailed representation of Jerusalem. It is amazingly similar to the Old City of today with many of the same gates, the Cardo or main street, and churches referred to in Christian literature. Fourteen centuries later the mosaic map confirms the presence of Christianity and the importance of Jerusalem as the "center of the earth."

Ten minutes away by car is Mount Nebo, an early Christian pilgrimage site memorializing the spot where Moses passed leadership to Joshua. A basilica with Byzantine mosaics and a platform to see what Moses saw when he could not enter the promised land are features of the promontory.

Christian Communities

Eastern Orthodox Christians in Jordan are related to parishes of the Greek Orthodox Patriarchate of Jerusalem.

There are three communities of Oriental Orthodox churches in Jordan: churches related to the Armenian Apostolic Patriarchate of Jerusalem as well as parishes of the Syriac Orthodox Church and the Coptic Orthodox Church.

The Catholic family of churches is represented by the Greek Catholic (Melkite) Church, the Armenian Catholic Church, and parishes belonging to the Latin Patriarchate of Jerusalem.

The Evangelical family includes Anglican parishes related to the Episcopal Church in Jerusalem and the Middle East and a parish of the Evangelical Lutheran Church in Jordan and the Holy Land. In addition, there are Evangelical parishes related to the Christian and Missionary Alliance, the Assemblies of God, the Church of the Nazarene, the Seventh-day Adventist Church, Baptist churches, and Free Evangelical and Bible Preaching churches.

Christian Population

The Christian population in Jordan is estimated to be about 150,000, more than half of whom are Greek Orthodox. Another third are Greek and Latin Catholics. Protestant, Armenian, and Syriac Orthodox communities are relatively small but influential. Some of the congregations have welcomed refugees from the recent turmoil in Iraq into their midst and have provided a variety of humanitarian services to these people.

Historical Background

Ever since the formation of the state, Christians have been constitutionally guaranteed freedom of worship and religious education as well as a representation in parliament that is disproportionately larger than their numbers in society.

Most Jordanian Christians are of Palestinian origin (as is at least half of the Muslim population). Although many of these Christians arrived in the kingdom as refugees in 1948 and 1967, they have been reasonably well absorbed into the society. None, for example, live in the camps still maintained by the United Nations. Further immigration of Christians from the West Bank to Jordan, where many have been reunited with their families, is the reason that today there are more members of the Greek Orthodox community in Jordan than in Israel and Palestine. In 2002, however, Jordan closed its borders to Palestinians as a signal to Israel that it will not receive new refugees should they be forced to leave their homes. With the outbreak of the war between the coalition forces and Iraq, more than half a million Iraqi refugees fled to Jordan, including significant numbers of Christians. Although their future status is unclear — many are unlikely to return to Iraq — it is unlikely they will seek or be granted Jordanian citizenship. Most of these refugees seem to desire to emigrate to Scandinavia or other Western nations.

Contemporary Circumstances

The Hashemite family of King Abdullah II claims direct descent from the Prophet Muhammad. For this reason, its authority, within the kingdom and throughout the Muslim world, is highly respected. Although the values of Islam are officially affirmed, Jordan has been open to modernization based heavily on Western legal and educational models. *Shar'ia* law governs only family relations and the administration of religious property for Muslims.

There is a clear political desire (and one reflected in law and practice) to guarantee the political and religious rights of Christians, who constitute about 6 percent of the population. The balance of the five million Jordanians are Sunni Muslims. Although Christians may not seek converts among Muslims in Jordan, they are otherwise free to practice their faith, build churches, and run educational institutions. Weddings and funerals, along with other celebrations, are attended by people of a variety of religious affiliations, and urban neighborhoods are religiously diverse. Some Christians have faced difficulties in the courts, which generally are controlled by individual Muslims.

Well over half of the Christians in Jordan are part of the middle and upper classes and enjoy a high level of education. This has led to their strong participation in public administration and the professions. The Latin Catholic and Anglican communities are active in the society, especially in the educational and health fields. Because Christian schools and hospitals have become prestigious, the churches and their clergy make a significant impact on the social and political life of the nation.

King Abdullah, who succeeded to the Hashemite throne in February 1999, appears also to be inheriting the great attachment that Muslims and Christians alike had for his father, King Hussein. That affection was due in large part to King Hussein's efforts to strengthen the democratic and economic life of their small but strategic constitutional monarchy.

Christians and Muslims alike are generally well informed about regional politics, and are increasingly impatient with Israel's domination of the area. In 2009 they were awaiting with anticipation the creative involvement of the Obama Administration in the region.

Interfaith Activities

Jordan's Prince El Hassan Bin Talal is deeply interested in creating good relations between the religious groups, and the Royal Institute for Interfaith Studies operates under his patronage. He is the author of a frequently quoted book, *Christianity in the Arab World*. Because many areas of Jordan are completely or overwhelmingly Muslim, the institute frequently initiates discussion groups across economic and social lines to foster good relations.

Lebanon

The strategic location and unique ecumenical and interreligious experience of Lebanon, one of the smallest countries in the Arab world, have made it important above and beyond its size. Bordered by Syria on the north and east and by Israel on the south, the Lebanese Republic has been plagued by what its president once described as "the war of others on our land." In addition to its fertile Bekaa valley, Lebanon is known for its mountain fastness, where such diverse religious groups as Maronite Catholics, Shi'ite Muslims, and Druze have found safe havens. The capital, Beirut, is located on the coastal strip, where the mountains rise rapidly from the Mediterranean; its culture and economic prominence have earned it the designation of the Paris of the East.

Christian Communities

The Eastern Orthodox family of churches is represented in Lebanon mainly by Greek Orthodox parishes related to the Patriarchate of Antioch (located in Damascus). In addition to this strong church, there are very small Russian Orthodox communities related to the Moscow Patriarchate.

The Oriental Orthodox family is largely represented by the Armenian Apostolic Church, whose Catholicosate of Cilicia is located in the Beirut suburb of Antelias. In addition, there are also relatively small Syriac Orthodox and Coptic Orthodox communities.

The Catholic family of churches is dominated by the Maronite

Church of Antioch, whose Patriarchate of Antioch and All the East is located at Bkerke in the mountains north of Beirut. This church is numerically and historically the major Christian community in the country. Other Catholic communities in Lebanon include a relatively large Melkite (Greek Catholic) Church and smaller Armenian and Syrian Catholic bodies, as well as the Chaldean Church and Latin-rite Communities.

The Evangelical family of churches in Lebanon includes parishes of the National Evangelical Synod of Syria and Lebanon, the National Evangelical Churches of Lebanon, the Union of Armenian Evangelical Churches, and the Episcopal Church (in Jerusalem and the Middle East). Other Evangelical communities include two Baptist groups, the Church of God, Seventh-day Adventists, the Brethren Evangelical Church, the Church of the Friends, the Church of the Nazarene, the Evangelical Christian Alliance, and a number of independent missions.

Most of these Evangelical churches are gathered together, along with their counterparts in Syria, in the Supreme Council of the Evangelical Community in Syria and Lebanon. The Supreme Council is rooted in the *millet* system of the Ottoman Empire[1] and was legally accepted in 1850 and 1853 as the body representing Protestants. The French mandate (which covered what is now Lebanon and Syria following World War I) also recognized the Supreme Council as the basis for legal representation for Protestants.

Finally, there is a small community of the Assyrian Church of the East, a church not part of any of the four families of churches.

Christian Population

Christians now number about 39 percent of the total Lebanese population of nearly four million, although the collective role of Christians in the society remains even more significant. The total Maronite population is as large as that of all the other churches combined. Because of its size and history, it has played a major political and educational role in the country. The Greek Catholics (Melkites) also are relatively strong.

---

1. For further explanation of the *millet* system, see the boxed texts on pp. 54 and 115.

Dar Sayyidat ul-Jabal

The shrine of Dar Sayyidat ul-Jabal (Our Lady of the Mountain) was established in the early 1990s, and its fame rests not in its history as a site but rather on its importance as a modern piece of the history of Lebanon. The church appears to be a Phoenician ship turned over, reminding the Lebanese of their traditional ancestry in the Phoenicians who landed on the coast in the third millennium B.C. The ship is also a Christian symbol of the church, and this "ship" opens out into a soaring space as you walk down the aisle to the altar.

The nearby house was founded by the Maronite Sisters of the Holy Family in 1992 to be a rest home for retired sisters, a retreat for lay and clergy in need of rest, and a center for conferences. It is only twelve and a half miles from Beirut in the town of Fatqa overlooking Junieh Bay. On one side the view is of the Mediterranean Sea and on the other there is a panorama of the Lebanon mountains.

The Eastern Orthodox communities are second to the Catholic family in size. Members are served by four of the ten dioceses in the region of the Patriarchate of Antioch. Lebanon is home to several educational and monastic institutions of this Damascus-based patriarchate. The Armenian Apostolic Church enjoys a high visibility because of the presence of its active and distinguished catholicosate near Beirut, as well as because of its schools and churches. For many years the relatively modest Protestant community in Lebanon has provided strong ecumenical leadership; the Near East School of Theology (p. 182) in Beirut offers theological training for Protestants throughout the region.

Historical Background

In ancient times, Lebanon was famous for its wood (especially cedar) and for iron and copper. It was the home of Phoenician traders, who sailed the then-known world. During the Ottoman Empire and continuing until the present, the several religious communities were assigned responsibility for legal issues (including marriage and inheritance) within their own groups.

At the end of World War I, France gained control over most of Greater Syria and the League of Nations eventually granted it a mandate for both Syria and Lebanon. Lebanon was seen as a multiconfessional state and the religious communities were assigned certain political roles. Making up more than half the population at the time, Christians had a strong influence on the constitution that allocated powerful roles among Christians and Sunni Muslims. Seats in parliament and ministerial posts in government were also divided along religious lines. The creation of the State of Israel in 1948, however, was a destabilizing factor, as more than 100,000 Palestinians (mostly Muslim) arrived to live for generations as stateless refugees.

Two civil wars were fought as the demography of Lebanon changed, with Shi'ite Muslims claiming a larger role. The constant conflict on the southern border has continued, with Israeli air strikes reaching north even to Beirut. Although a Christian still retains the role of head of state, Christians no longer hold the majority of parliamentary seats. As the twenty-first century dawned, war-ravaged Beirut was being rebuilt and the country's economy showed signs of renewal and new vitality.

Contemporary Circumstances

The situation in Lebanon is regarded as particularly precarious by the General Secretary of the Middle East Council of Churches, Guirguis Ibrahim Saleh. "There is a general mood of despair, sadness and ambiguity at all levels," he says, "especially in the light of recent political events." He cites the battle in 2007 at the Nahr el Bared Palestinian refugee camp, and continuing frequent aerial attacks and car bombs, some in the parts of Beirut where Christians live. The country seems trapped in a struggle between Western powers and regional groups. The near future seems unclear, especially with economic stress, increasing unemployment, and continuing emigration.

The Christian communities themselves have been divided as a result of the civil strife. The Maronites have sought to maintain the intel-

Mary Mikhael, Pioneering Woman Theologian

Dr. Mary Mikhael is the first woman to become president of a seminary in the Middle East. She spent her teaching career in Lebanon after earning a Master and a Doctor of Education at Columbia University in New York. She has written countless articles related to theology and the position of women in the church along with chapters of books and studies for women. She has also lectured all over the U.S.A., Europe, and the Middle Eastern countries on the same subjects. Her work has also brought her to the attention of the Wider Church Ministries of the United Church of Christ, USA, on whose board she has served.

The Near East School of Theology is not known for its beauty or its history but for its special people and its history-making function. The Near East School of Theology in Beirut, Lebanon, is the only interdenominational Evangelical (Protestant) theological seminary in the Middle East that teaches in the English language. That is not a restriction because the forty-thousand-volume library contains books in English, Arabic, Armenian, French, and German, and the faculty come from all over the world. It was founded by the same group of missionaries who started American University in Beirut, and it continues its contacts with American (and other) denominations now as partners.

Under the guidance of Dr. Mikhail, the NEST, as it is fondly known, has become a community of Christians as well as an educational institution. Most of the students and faculty study, worship, and live together in one building in the Hamra section of Beirut, Lebanon. The nickname of NEST truly describes the sense of community and its importance in nurturing the future leadership of the Evangelical churches of the Middle East, including Arabs, Armenians, Africans, and other ethnic groups.

lectual and economic prominence they had gained under the French as well as their central role in society. Other churches, especially those with ties to Syrian-based patriarchates, have been more accepting of Arab (including Palestinian) influences and have been more critical of Israeli policies and bombardments.

Christians are still debating whether to continue with the 1943 constitution designating roles and percentages to religious communities, or to honor the 1990 agreement that ended the war but also demanded secularization of the political system and a majority rule. Many Christians are concerned that majority rule could mean the imposition of Muslim laws in which their rights could be curtailed. In 1997, however, the nation experienced an unusual degree of unity when the visit of Pope John Paul II was greeted warmly by Muslims as well as Christians. Nevertheless, one area of tension involves efforts of some churches or individual Christians to proselytize Muslims, especially children. In 2002 a missionary nurse from the U.S. was killed by Muslim extremists who resented her efforts to convert youngsters.

The Middle East Council of Churches, which maintains its major office in Beirut, has attempted to bridge religious and social gaps, helping the country to restore its pluralism as the basis for democracy. The MECC also has sought to provide a witness to reconciliation, justice, and peace as the basis for equality, freedom, and human dignity. In the midst of tension, acute frustration, and war the churches associated with the council have demonstrated their desire for Christian unity and peaceful solutions to difficult problems. Through the council they have organized service ministries and human rights efforts and have been unequivocal in their opposition to the country's warlords and the violence that has wracked the country.

Interfaith Activities

The principal churches of Lebanon acknowledge the hardship and grief that both Christians and Muslims have caused each other and have initiated steps toward reconciliation with both Muslims and Jews. Having lived together for nearly thirteen hundred years — sometimes happily and sometimes not — the Christians and Muslims have had on-the-ground experience as neighbors. Some leaders call this the "dialogue of life." With an emphasis on overcoming the effects of the long civil war, Christians and Muslims both sense the urgency and the need for a defined purpose. An organized "Arab Working Group on Muslim-Christian Dialogue" is proactively seeking a civil society in which members of both religious groups share equally in citizenship, have equal access to impartial law, and discover that respect and understanding can lead to the enrichment of the culture they share. An "Arab Muslim-Christian Covenant" has been developed that describes the values and basis for what it calls "a culture of dialogue." Two other groups have functioned in this area: the Lebanese Christian-Muslim Committee for Dialogue and a Lebanese Forum for Dialogue. Members of these groups believe progress has been made and that they need to share their experiences, especially in schools and universities, in order to impact the next generation.

The Maghreb (North Africa)

Although Africa north of the Sahara is not generally considered part of the Middle East, the history and Arab character of nations such as Algeria and Tunisia place it logically (if not geographically) within the purview of this book. The nations themselves relate closely to the Middle Eastern states since they share much of the same history and culture and many of the same problems. Like most of the Middle East, Algeria and Tunisia were integral to the story of the early church as it spread along the shores of the Mediterranean; sadly, they share the decline of Christianity with the region as well.

The People's Democratic Republic of Algeria is the second largest country on the African continent, while the smallest country in what is known as the Maghreb (Arab northern Africa) is the Tunisian Republic, where the ancient city of Carthage was the doorway through which Christianity moved in the third century. Among the early Christian leaders in the region were such notables as Augustine, Cyprian, and Tertullian, who first observed that the "blood of the martyrs is the seed of the church." The Christian communities in both countries are today very small (approximately 1 percent of the population). The conciliar Evangelical churches there hold formal membership in the Middle East Council of Churches, and little is known of the scattered churches in the other countries of the Maghreb (Libya, Morocco, and Mauritania).

Christian Communities

The Eastern Orthodox family is represented throughout the Maghreb by a few Greek Orthodox parishes associated with the Patriarchate of Alexandria and All Africa. There are scattered congregations with ties to the Moscow Patriarchate as well.

The Oriental Orthodox family has Coptic Orthodox parishes in Libya and Algeria, as well as an Armenian Apostolic and a Syriac Orthodox congregation in Algeria.

The Catholic family has Latin-rite parishes that dominate the Christian communities in Algeria and Morocco. In Libya there are only a few Roman (Latin) Catholics but there are Coptic and Greek Catholic parishes there too. In Algeria there are also Maronite, Syriac, and Greek Catholic (Melkite) congregations.

The Evangelical family includes Anglican parishes in Algeria, Libya, Morocco, and Tunisia. There are Protestant congregations with French Reformed roots in Algeria and congregations with British Methodist origins in Tunisia, and there are independent or nondenominational groups, including Assemblies of God, Baptists, Evangelical Bible missions, and Seventh-day Adventists, in Algeria, Libya, Morocco, and Tunisia. Many if not most of the Evangelical churches serve mainly expatriates and occasional tourists.

Of all the churches in the Maghreb, only the groups with Methodist and Reformed backgrounds participate directly in the Middle East Council of Churches. The Orthodox and Catholic parishes relate ecumenically through the patriarchates or churches of which they are a part.

Christian Population

Throughout the Maghreb, the Christian population is relatively very small. In Algeria and Morocco the Latin-rite Catholics were estimated some years ago to be more than 90 percent of all Christians in those countries. In Algeria, the Catholic population peaked at nearly one million, most of whom returned to France following Algerian independence in 1962. Other expatriates left following the murder of Bishop Pierre Claverie of Oran in 1996. In the meantime Protestants, especially non-conciliar evangelicals, grew rapidly, making Algeria the country where Christianity is growing faster than any other place in the Arab world. As might be expected since the country borders Egypt, the Coptic Orthodox have more than 80 percent of all Christians in Libya.

Historical Background

Each country in the area has its own history, especially since the mid-nineteenth century. These countries had once been part of the Roman Empire (which facilitated the early spread of Christianity), and from later periods, after Islam swept the area, there is heavy Moorish and Ottoman influence. During the European colonialism of the nineteenth century, France became dominant in Morocco, Algeria, and Tunisia. French is still the second language, often used in business, even though each of the countries became fiercely independent following World War II. Libya had been invaded by Italy just prior to World War I and became independent in 1951; Italian is the second language there.

Nationalist fervor swept the entire area following World War II when the Germans and Italians were driven out by the Allies. Independence was won by each nation only following intense struggles. That was especially true in Algeria. As a result, the largely foreign Christian churches frequently are perceived as the tools or at least the remnants of colonial powers. Because of that perception, the rights of even the indigenous Arab-speaking Christians sometimes have been seriously compromised.

Contemporary Circumstances

The overwhelming majority of the people throughout the North African countries are Sunni Muslims. Because proselytism is against the law nearly everywhere in the area, church membership is largely made up of expatriates. Although laws protect Christians in most countries, extremists or nationalist groups have sometimes targeted churches and religious leaders. A priest and a nun who were responsible for a library in a poor Algerian neighborhood were killed in the 1980s. Soon thereafter four White Fathers (members of a Roman Catholic order) were gunned down at their home. On the day the priests were buried, however, the city shut down and the residents lined the road to the cemetery to honor their work for justice. Seven Trappist monks were kidnapped and beheaded in 1996, and an outspoken Catholic bishop was assassinated by a group that used a remote-controlled car bomb. The general population, however, reacted quickly with verbal and other support of the Christians.

From the colonial period onward both Protestants and Catholics in Algeria have had access to radio broadcasts. Weekly programs have given way to less frequent broadcasts, now usually in relation to Christian holidays. The churches considered discontinuing this public witness but decided to continue it as a way of affirming the increasingly open, tolerant, and pluralistic social patterns. Sometimes the programs take the form of roundtable discussions in which Muslim theologians also participate. The public visibility of the churches in the area, however, is at best limited and uncommon. In 2006 an ordinance and an executive decree in Algeria defined permissible religious meetings and imposed criminal penalties for any infraction. During the following three years there were no known infractions.

Nevertheless, by the end of the twentieth century there was enough stability in Algeria for very modest church growth, and this was viewed by the Christian population as a cause for quiet hope and guarded optimism.

Interfaith Activities

It is difficult for so small a minority to engage the much larger majority in common activities or dialogue. However, as the nations of the Maghreb — especially Algeria, Morocco, and Tunisia — become more democratic and as the educational level increases, the Islamic majority is clearly more tolerant. On occasion, as when the Catholic monks and bishop were brutally killed or when a church was defaced, Muslim officials have intentionally paid condolence visits to the Christian community. On one occasion, the rector of the Grand Mosque in Paris publicly sent his secretary with a message of solidarity. Although many Christians have good relations with Muslim friends and acquaintances, there is little formal dialogue or common religious enterprise.

The Persian Gulf and Saudi Arabia

The countries of the Persian Gulf are much in the news because of their strategic military importance, as well as the reliance of Western industrial nations on the petroleum resources of the area. Yet the oil-dependent nations, including those in North America, seem uninterested in the human situation in the Gulf, except as they worry about its potential for violence. Much has been made of Iraq's intransigent behavior, but too little is known about the roots of that behavior or how Western sanctions, massive bombing, and years of war have affected the people of Iraq. Even less is known about the conditions facing migrant laborers in other Gulf states or, indeed, that significant numbers of those workers are Christians. The religious dynamics in Saudi Arabia, Kuwait, Bahrain, the United Arab Emirates, Qatar, Yemen, and Oman have been greatly affected because of these issues.

Christian Communities

In the Gulf area, most of the congregations serve the large numbers of expatriate workers from Asian, African, Western, and other Middle Eastern countries.

The Eastern Orthodox family is represented by Greek Orthodox communities in Kuwait, Oman, and the United Arab Emirates. Many of the members of these churches are Arab workers from Palestine, Jordan, Lebanon, and Syria.

The Oriental Orthodox are more varied. Two Indian Orthodox

groups can be found in each of the countries along the Gulf: the Syriac "Jacobite" Indian Church related to the Patriarchate of Damascus and an independent Syriac church also known as the Malankara Orthodox. As the presence of those churches suggests, there are large numbers of migrant workers from nearby India. In addition, there are Armenian Apostolic and Coptic Orthodox churches in Kuwait and Armenian and Ethiopian Orthodox churches in the United Arab Emirates.

The Catholic family is the largest Christian community in the Gulf. This group includes Latin-rite churches related to two dioceses: the Vicarate Apostolic of Kuwait has congregations in Kuwait, and the Vicarate Apostolic of Arabia has parishes in Bahrain, Oman, Qatar, Yemen, and the Emirates. In Saudi Arabia, Catholics — like all Christians — worship privately or even underground. There also are Armenian, Chaldean, Coptic, Greek (Melkite), and Maronite communities in Kuwait. Syriac Catholics have small congregations in both Bahrain and Kuwait. Throughout the Gulf area (with the exception of Kuwait), Catholics are served, in English, by Capuchin priests except when visiting clergy are present. In Kuwait, Carmelite Franciscan priests provide services except when a visiting priest is present. In addition, Catholic nuns are present in Bahrain, the Emirates, and Yemen, where they are engaged in educational work. Most Catholic faithful are from India and the Philippines.

The Evangelical family includes Anglican parishes in Bahrain, Kuwait, Qatar, and the Emirates. Those parishes are related to the Episcopal diocese of Cyprus and the Gulf (Province of Jerusalem and the Middle East). Protestant communities established by the Reformed Church in America are present in Bahrain and Oman. The Oman church is a shared chaplaincy with the Episcopal diocese. The languages spoken by members of those churches suggest their international character: Arabic, English, Malayalam, Tamil, Telugu, Urdu, Korean, and Tagalog.

In addition, Protestants from India are served by Mar Thoma parishes in Bahrain, Kuwait, Oman, Qatar, and the Emirates; there also are parishes related to the Church of South India in Bahrain, Kuwait, Oman, Qatar, and the Emirates. The German Lutheran Church has parishes throughout the Gulf that meet occasionally when a circuit-riding pastor visits from Cyprus. Nondenominational parishes related to the Church of Pakistan are located in Bahrain, Kuwait, Oman, and the Emirates. The Brethren Assembly has parishes in Bahrain, Kuwait,

Oman, and the Emirates, and the Assemblies of God has congregations in Bahrain and the Emirates. A Seventh-day Adventist congregation is located in Kuwait. The St. Thomas Evangelical Church has parishes in Bahrain and Kuwait. There also are small to moderate-sized pentecostal congregations and a variety of "full gospel" and fundamentalist groups worshiping in various places throughout the Gulf area. In several Gulf states there are Norwegian and British missions to seamen.

Christian Population

Christians constitute between 5 and 10 percent of the total population in most countries of the Gulf area, although reliable demographic data is unavailable. The great majority of the Christian population, however, is drawn from the foreign workers, who vastly outnumber the local populations in Kuwait, Qatar, and the United Arab Emirates and who represent more than a third of the total in Bahrain and Saudi Arabia. The majority of the workers come from Asia, with the largest numbers from India and the Philippines. It is estimated that the total Christian population in the Gulf is between one and two million; of these, fewer than one thousand are indigenous people.

The largest Christian community is in Saudi Arabia, but worship there is unofficial or even secret. Very little is known about the circumstances of these Christians. Professor Johan Gäarde, a Swedish researcher, points to the dramatic increase of Christians in Saudi Arabia, from a mere 50 in 1900 to 789,065 in 2005. According to the MECC, however, they live under strict surveillance and are not permitted to show outward signs of their being Christian.

Many of the congregations in the Gulf area are relatively small and are often quite transient. Worshipers are said to have "one foot in the Gulf and the other foot back home"; they frequently consider themselves to be "just passing through." This complicates efforts to estimate the number of Christians.

Some congregations serving temporary workers from Asia are quite large, however. In Qatar, the Catholic parish has been swelled by nearly sixty thousand migrants, many from India, while in Oman the churches are struggling to accommodate and communicate with a wide variety of ethnic groups in which many of the workers have been affiliated with pentecostal movements. In Dubai, one of the seven United Arab Emirates, eighty thousand Catholics are associated with a single parish where only a few priests are allowed work permits. Anglican parishes in the Gulf and Arabian Peninsula frequently host groups from other Christian traditions. At Holy Trinity Dubai, for example, as many as 35,000 persons enter the front gate each week to worship on the property. The Anglican archdeaconry for the Gulf also offers a mission to seafarers based both in Dubai and in Fujairah. In Kuwait there are an estimated forty thousand Egyptian workers; the Coptic Orthodox presence there is strong.

Historical Background

The states lining the Persian Gulf are largely desert lands where the early settlers depended mainly on fishing and pearl hunting for their livelihood. The Gulf was also a major trade route between East and West, and by the eighth century its western coast had become a trade and financial center linking Baghdad with India and China. After the sixteenth century, European merchants, especially the Portuguese and British, were influential. Catholic and Anglican churches, among others, arrived to serve the expatriates who settled in the region. The discovery of oil in the twentieth century led to rapid changes from a traditional to a modern society in which wealth became a dominant factor. To meet the needs for labor, a great many foreign migrant workers were brought in, including persons with a wide variety of religious backgrounds.

According to tradition, the Apostle Bartholomew brought Christianity to Arabia. The specific reference in the book of Acts to Arabs among those present for the first Pentecost may point to a substantial Christian population in the area. By A.D. 325 Arab bishops were present at the Council of Nicea. Later, during the Islamic period, missionaries arrived from Europe and America. In addition to Catholics and Anglicans, the Reformed Church in America played a significant role by providing a Christian witness throughout the Gulf area through medical care and education as well as spiritual nurture. Following the rapid growth of the Gulf region after the discovery of oil, these churches also engaged in advocacy on behalf of the workers' well-being.

Contemporary Circumstances

Significant changes are taking place in this area as the governments recognize the need for services to foreign workers and realize that the churches are equipped to meet some of those needs. The Vatican nuncio, Guiseppe de Andrea, brings to his post a long personal involvement with migrant issues. Because the social, as well as religious, needs of the workers are so great, the Middle East Council of Churches has helped the established churches to minister more intentionally to the various ethnic groups. It works in a collaborative style, engaging in efforts with several regional ecumenical councils, the World Council of Churches, the National Council of Churches in the Philippines, and various UN and nongovernmental agencies.

Proselytizing the local population is forbidden and the churches need governmental approval for places of worship, visas for clergy and staff, and permission to import Bibles and religious material. The United Bible Societies play a significant role. Oman and Qatar have authorized several church buildings during the last decade. In Dubai, one of the Emirates, a church compound has been developed where thousands of Christians meet in Catholic, Orthodox, and Protestant churches.

In recent years the Emir of Bahrain has received church representatives several times to discuss their concerns, and in 2000 he invited the Ecumenical Patriarch of Constantinople to make a formal visit. Along with Kuwait, Bahrain has established diplomatic relations with the Vatican. In the Kingdom of Saudi Arabia, the right of non-Muslims to worship privately has been acknowledged by senior government officials. In April 2001, the Saudi foreign ministry told the UN Committee on Human Rights that "non-Muslims enjoy full freedom to engage in their religious observances in private."

Since September 11, 2001, the churches in the Gulf have prayed for peace regularly. United services in several locations were arranged during the Week of Prayer for Christian Unity and these often focused on the urgent need for peacemaking, especially in Asia, Africa, and the Middle East.

Interfaith Activities

In several Gulf states a significant Muslim-Christian encounter is taking place. At an Islamic Conference in Doha in 2000, messages were invited from several Orthodox churches. During the visit by the Ecumenical Patriarch of Constantinople to Bahrain, Beit al-Qur'an (the House of the Qu'ran) organized conversations with Christians; the Archbishop of Canterbury also spoke there, asking, "How far can we travel together?" When the Archbishop visited Qatar on the same visit, the country's ruler stressed the importance of coexistence and dialogue. At about the same time, Kuwait's Information Ministry invited the Reverend Lewis Scudder representing the Middle East Council of Churches to give a public lecture on Muslim-Christian relations. At Al-Amana Center in Oman, historically related to the Reformed Church in America, Christian-Muslim dialogue and church unity have become major agenda items.

One problem that has surfaced in these conversations is the strain on positive relationships caused by the involvement of several evangelical and pentecostal movements from Asia and the United States. Well-funded and organized campaigns have attempted an active outreach to non-Christians. The local governments tend to hold the long-established churches responsible for what all Christians do in the community. In the Emirates, three American "missionaries" several years ago were arrested for handing out materials on the street. In addition, most of the expatriate Christians themselves are more concerned about ministering to their own people than becoming involved in the needed dialogue with other religions and cultures — including local and foreign Muslims as well as Buddhists, Hindus, and Sikhs, who have come as migrant workers.

Sudan

The Republic of the Sudan, the largest country in Africa, is a complex and suffering nation. It is neither fully Arab nor completely African. Like Egypt, its northern neighbor, Sudan is dependent upon the Nile, which flows from the humid tropical forests in the south to the arid deserts in the north. Seventy-one percent of its forty million people live in rural areas where cotton and gum arabic are the principal products. A divided nation, Sudan is torn between cultural imperatives and be-deviled by a civil war that began the year before its independence in 1956 and has continued except for a respite of just over ten years. With international assistance a comprehensive peace agreement was signed in 2005, granting Southern Sudan autonomy for six years, after which a referendum for independence was promised.

Sudan has one of the most diverse populations in Africa. Literally hundreds of ethnic, tribal, and language groups make political collabo-ration very difficult. A separate conflict broke out in the western re-gion of Darfur in 2003. Two million people were displaced as a result of the fighting, with many persons, especially women and girls, suffering from rape and death. Starvation and illness were prevalent and the cen-tral government was widely blamed for permitting or planning geno-cide. Peace keeping forces have struggled to stabilize the situation.

Although Sudan would not normally be considered part of the Middle East, it is included in this book because the Christian churches there historically have been related to the Middle East Council of Churches.

Christian Communities

In the Sudan, the Eastern Orthodox family of churches is represented by several parishes related to the Patriarchate of Alexandria and All Africa. These are located mainly in the northern part of the country.

In addition to the Coptic Orthodox Church, the Oriental Orthodox family of churches includes parishes related to the Ethiopian Orthodox and Armenian Apostolic Churches. These also are located principally in the northern part of the country.

The Catholic family is represented by large numbers of Roman Catholics and by small congregations of Melkites and Maronites. The Catholic communities are largely in the southern part of Sudan, where Sudanese Christians live as a minority among believers in animist religions.

The Evangelical family includes the Episcopal Church and two Presbyterian bodies: the Presbyterian Church of the Sudan and the Evangelical Church in Sudan. Most of their communicants also live in the south. The following Protestant groups are not members of the conciliar movement in Sudan: the Church of East Central Sudan, the Sudanese Church of Christ, the Evangelical Revival Church, the Seventh-day Adventist Church, an independent Baptist Church, and a number of non-denominational congregations.

Christian Population

Christians are reported to make up less than 20 percent of the Sudanese population. The largest groups are Roman Catholics, Episcopalians, and Presbyterians. For the most part, these communicants live in the southern part of the country, where there are many different ethnic groups and where Christianity is growing rapidly among indigenous peoples.

Roger Schrock, who served from September 1990 to May 1995 as executive for the New Sudan Council of Churches, described the rapid growth of the "suffering . . . persecuted" church in the Sudan in the March-April 1997 issue of the MECC *NewsReport*. He cited the growth of the Episcopal Diocese of Rumbek from 9 congregations to 357 during the decade ending in 1993. One Presbyterian pastor, just graduated from seminary, baptized 9,288 persons in a single year. Schrock also quoted the Sudanese ambassador to Britain as saying, "Our government's goal to produce an Islamic society has been a failure. At no time in Sudan's history has the church grown as rapidly as it has in the 1990s." Rapid growth continued in the early years of the twenty-first century, when the Episcopal Church developed so rapidly that four dioceses grew to twenty-seven. The Presbyterian Church also has continued to grow very rapidly.

Historical Background

Ancient northern Sudan was under Egyptian domination during much of its history. Christianity was introduced from Egypt and Ethiopia and by the sixth century A.D. the church was well established in the Kingdom of Kush, which covered what is now northern Sudan. With the spread of Islam, the church was destroyed and the population became Muslim. The last of the Nubian kings converted to Islam in the seventeenth century. Christianity was reintroduced by the modern Western mission movement during the nineteenth century, largely among the non-Arab peoples of southern Sudan.

The complex communal strife between the northern and southern parts of the Sudan dates back to a British colonial policy that sought to avoid confrontation with the Arab north by maintaining the status quo there. At the same time the British opened the south to Christian missionary efforts. English became the language of instruction in church-related schools and this further separated the groups. A "divide and conquer" policy exacerbated ethnic differences.

Contemporary Circumstances

In the first phase of the civil war (1958-1964) several military regimes pursued a policy of Arabization and Islamization in the south and expelled foreign missionaries. A decade of peace (1972-1982) was brokered by the World Council of Churches and the All Africa Council of Churches. The agreement gave autonomy to the southern region and confirmed equality under the law for Muslims, Christians, and the followers of traditional religions. The conflict flared again, however, when the central government failed to improve economic problems in the south and threatened to siphon off potential oil revenues. The central authorities also sought to impose the Islamic *shar'ia* law on the whole country. By 1994 the continuing warfare forced the central government to accept the mediation of the Inter-Government Authority on Development (IGAD). A negotiated "Declaration of Principles" was based on recognition of Sudan's pluralistic character. In 2005 a Comprehensive Peace Agreement was signed granting regional autonomy with a promise of a referendum on independence. In 2010 many Southern Sudanese seemed to look forward to a state of their own.

The impact of the conflict in Sudan is impossible to overestimate. Between three and five million Sudanese have been displaced from their homes with nearly a million of the displaced persons living as refugees in bordering countries. Estimates of deaths attributable to the war reach as high as 1.5 million persons. Slavery has flourished, with an estimated nine thousand persons taken into the north from southern Sudan and the Nuba mountain region.

In 1996 the churches of Sudan published a statement entitled "Here We Stand: United in Action for Peace," identifying their calling within the society, their vision for Sudan's future, and five practical steps that must be taken to achieve peace. With partners abroad, the churches are working ecumenically as they minister to acute human needs.

Interfaith Activities

The years of civil strife, the sharp regional division between the Muslim north and the Animist/Christian south, and the historic presence of dozens of ethnic and tribal groups have made rational interfaith efforts very difficult. Through the Middle East Council of Churches and the World Council of Churches, however, the churches of Sudan are seeking to extend their peacemaking initiatives and have opened lines of communication in the region to both Sunni and Shi'ite Muslim leaders.

Syria

Home to one of the most ancient peoples on earth, Syria often has been the battleground for hostile and greedy powers. Many of the outsiders, including Western crusaders, left behind citadels and fortresses; today these stand as mute reminders of Syria's violent past. Damascus, the capital, is probably the world's oldest continuously inhabited city. In biblical times, a Jew with Roman citizenship was traveling along a major trade route outside Damascus when he was converted to Christianity and became the apostle Paul. The present national borders of the Syrian Arab Republic were drawn after World War I during the period of the French mandate.

Christian Communities

Eastern Orthodox Christians in Syria are related to parishes of the Greek Orthodox Patriarchate of Antioch and All the East, whose see is in Damascus.

Oriental Orthodox Christians are related to the Syriac Orthodox Patriarchate of Antioch and All the East, whose see is also in Damascus, and to the Armenian Apostolic Catholicosate of Cilicia.

Members of the Catholic family are related to the Greek Catholic (Melkite) Patriarchate of Antioch and All the East, whose see is in Damascus, and to Maronite, Chaldean, Latin-rite, Syriac Catholic, and Armenian Catholic churches.

The Evangelical family includes parishes related to the National Evangelical Synod of Syria and Lebanon and to the Union of Armenian

Evangelical Churches in the Near East. The Evangelical churches in Syria that are not part of the MECC include parishes related to the Christian and Missionary Alliance, the Church of God, the Church of the Nazarene, Armenian Brethren, Seventh-day Adventist, and Assemblies of God, as well as several independent congregations. The Supreme Council of the Evangelical Community in Syria and Lebanon functions as the *millet* for most of the evangelical churches of Syria as well as those in Lebanon.[1]

There are also communities related to the Ancient Assyrian Church of the East, which is not a part of any of the church families.

Christian Population

The Christian population in Syria is estimated at between 900,000 and 1,500,000, or up to 10 percent of the total population, not including an estimated 80,000 Iraqi refugees who are Christians. (In 2009 Syria was host to an estimated one and a half million refugees from Iraq.) About half of all Christians in Syria are Greek Orthodox. The Greek Catholic (Melkite) and the Armenian Apostolic churches each claim more than 110,000 members. The Syriac Orthodox Church has approximately 90,000 communicants. The Ancient Assyrian Church of the East has a significant community, as do the Syriac and Armenian Catholic churches. The various Protestant communities, together, include more than 20,000 believers.

Historical Background

Damascus was the center of Islamic civilization in the eighth and ninth centuries, when the Umayyad caliphs administered Islam's presence throughout the Middle East, across North Africa to Spain in the West, and to Persia and the borders of India in the East. Under the tolerant Umayyads, the Syrian population was mostly Christian. That demography continued into the fourteenth century, when the misguided crusader kingdom fell.

1. See the section on Lebanon, pp. 178ff., for more information. For more on the *millet* system, see pp. 54 and 115 above.

St. George Monastery of Homeyra

Monasteries named St. George (or El Khader, Jirjis, Gerias) abound in the Middle East. This particular monastery is near the "tourist trail" of the old Roman Highway and only a few miles from the famous Krak des Chevaliers. The area is called the Christian Valley or Wadi An-Nassara of Syria because it still contains many old villages that are completely Christian. The monastery was built in the sixth century during the time of Justinian with a second floor constructed during the Crusades. There also is a nineteenth-century church. It is a good place to compare the architectural features of the various centuries and to view the magnificent iconostasis (icon wall) at the front of the church. About fifteen monks live at the monastery and teach Byzantine chanting. They sing in the old church and there are also CDs and tapes available.

The nearby Krak des Chevaliers is also worth mentioning. It is a fine example of a crusader castle and a reminder that part of the motivation for the Crusades was the opening up of a safe pilgrimage route to Jerusalem and the Holy Land. The castles were to protect pilgrims and provide safe lodging along the way.

The Ottoman Turks dominated Syria from the sixteenth century until the end of World War I. At that time the dream of Arab nationalism gave rise to the first call for secular political government in the region. The Arab revolt from 1916 to 1918, headed by Prince Faisal bin Hussein, promoted an Arab government that sought justice and equality for Muslim, Christian, and Jewish residents. In the settlement following World War I, however, Britain and France were granted mandates in the region.

The twenty-five years of French control in Syria saw numerous violent rebellions — thirty-five in 1922 alone. Following independence and elections in 1947, a struggle for national and regional pan-Arab leadership lasted until 1966, when the thirteenth coup brought Colonel Hafiz al-Assad and two other members of his Ba'ath party to power. Eventually Colonel Assad forced his colleagues aside and, following a popular referendum in 1970, he became president. He continued that role until his death in July 2000, despite challenges from militant Islamic groups at home and rivalry with the radical wing of his party in Iraq. His leadership also was threatened by the regional destabilization related to the wars in which Israel occupied the Golan Heights and southern Lebanon as well as the West Bank and Gaza. When Bashar al-Assad, an ophthalmologist and soldier, succeeded his father as president there were few visible changes in policy.

Contemporary Circumstances

Since 1920, when Syria first declared (but failed for twenty-five years to achieve) independence from foreign domination, the country has respected all religions. Today the secular ideology of the Syrian Ba'ath party dominates; the only mention of Islam in the constitution is that the Head of State must be a Muslim. In an authoritarian political setting Syria's Christian communities are supervised by the government, but the government does give them freedom to buy land and build churches and pastoral buildings with the help of the state. The churches manage their own financial assets and the clergy are not civil servants. The government provides churches, as well as mosques and public institutions, with electricity and water.

Christians practice their faith openly. During Christian holy days (as during Muslim feasts) religious services are broadcast on Syrian television. Characterized as a tolerant land of friendly and generous people, Syria has become home to many who experienced religious persecution elsewhere: Armenians, Assyrians, Chaldeans, Suryanis, and others, most recently refugees from Iraq. Religion is not a factor in Syria's civil administration. All citizens are equal before the law and religious groups are guaranteed an opportunity for self-development. Christians participate in all areas of public life in Syria, including the Parliament.

Strong ecumenical programs for youth, women, Christian families, and refugees are operated through the Middle East Council of Churches, which maintains some of its program offices in Syria.

Interfaith Activities

Relationships between the churches and the three groups of Muslims in Syria are good. The three groups include Sunnis (who are estimated to represent 75 percent of the population), the Alawites (11 percent), and the Ismailis (1 percent). In addition, Druze communities are estimated at about 3 percent of the total population. Tiny Jewish communities are located in Damascus, Aleppo, and Al Qamish. In addition some 20,000 Israeli settlers live in the Golan Heights, which Israel has occupied since 1967. These settlers live in their own villages among an equal number of Arabs.

Important encounters between church and Islamic leaders are encouraged by the MECC. Muslim leaders, especially the Grand Mufti, whose headquarters are in Damascus, welcome contact with both Syrian and international Christian officials. He and the Grand Mufti of Aleppo cite a passage from the Qur'an: "[We] have made you nations and tribes, that you may know one another" (49:13).

Interfaith marriage is a problem, however. In the absence of civil marriage, only marriages between two Christians are registered as Christian. Both Muslim-Muslim and Christian-Muslim marriages are recorded as Muslim.

Turkey

In several ways the Republic of Turkey provides a bridge. Literally, the spans and ferries across the Bosporus link Europe and Asia. Because it looks West, its cities — especially Istanbul — have a mixture of European and Eastern cultures. Turkey also provides a bridge across the centuries. Its early Christian communities were crucial to the expansion of the ancient church and to the definition of Christian belief. From Constantinople, the center of the Byzantine Empire, Orthodox faith and piety spread especially in the north to Russia and the Balkans and west as far as Europe and the Americas. Today Turkey is officially a secular republic, but its Sunni Muslim majority sets the religious tone.

Christian Communities

The Eastern Orthodox family is represented by the Greek Orthodox Church (the Ecumenical Patriarchate) and the Bulgarian Orthodox Church.

The Oriental Orthodox family is comprised of the Armenian Apostolic Orthodox Church (Patriarchate of Constantinople) and the Syriac Orthodox Church.

The Catholic family includes Latin, Armenian, Syriac, Chaldean, and Greek (Melkite) Catholics.

The Evangelical family includes the Turkish Presbyterian Church and the Armenian Evangelical Union as well as the Seventh-day Adventist Church, the Korean Missionary Fellowship, the Turkish Orthodox

---

Cappadocia, Turkey

The landscape looks somewhat lunar as you drive into Cappadocia, but then you realize that it is a field of cones, sometimes with tilted hats. The so-called "Fairy Chimneys" are the result of volcanic eruptions millions of years ago followed by coursing water and wind erosion. Thousands of cones made of volcanic tuff were formed. Long before the time of Christ people began to carve out homes and villages in these cones, and Roman persecutions and invasion by Asian tribes made them a haven for ancient refugees. Today many of the rock dwellings have been turned into small shops.

Christians fleeing persecution developed monasteries and carved more than thirty-five hundred churches from the soft tuff. After the stone hardened in the air, the rooms and dwellings were painted. Churches have been dated by their frescoes from the ninth century onward. The interiors range from small solitary rooms for anchorite monks to large multi-room churches. Several cones are carved with an upper floor reached by hand and toe holds. Even pillows and chairs were created by carving the tuff. The outside geography is a wonder of nature; the inside a wonder of church art.

Church, and various fellowships serving refugees and displaced persons. There also are three expatriate groups: the Union Church of Istanbul, the German Evangelical Church in Istanbul, and Anglican chaplaincies in Istanbul, Izmir, and Ankara.

Christian Population

The Christian community in Turkey is a very small percentage of the total population. A consistent estimate is 0.2 percent of the nation's more than seventy-seven million people. The vast majority of all Christians now live in Istanbul itself, a city with a population of over twelve million. Residual communities throughout Anatolia (the land mass also called Asia Minor) include the churches and monasteries of the

Syriac Orthodox Archbishopric of Turabdin in southeastern Turkey, scattered Armenian and Catholic congregations, and Eastern Orthodox congregations in Antakya and Mersin that are related to the Patriarchate of Antioch and All the East.

The Ecumenical Patriarchate of Constantinople is accorded primacy of honor by all Christian groups in Turkey, although there are no more than three thousand Greek Orthodox Christians remaining in the country; most Greek Orthodox parish churches and institutions are closed. Of particular sadness is that their seminary at Halki, on one of the Princes' Islands in the Marmara Sea, remains closed by order of the Turkish government. Nevertheless, His All Holiness Patriarch Bartholomew is a courageous and important presence in the worldwide church. A Lenten encyclical issued in 2010 by Patriarch Bartholomew stressed the importance of Christian unity and echoed an encyclical written 90 years earlier by one of Bartholomew's predecessors. That 1920 letter, according to Olav Fykse Tveit, general secretary of the World Council of Churches, "provided a major impulse for the formation of the World Council."

In Istanbul there are some 60,000 Armenian Orthodox and about 2,500 Syriac Orthodox. The Armenians have a patriarchate and some twenty parishes, a very large hospital and retirement home, and other community enterprises. Most of the Armenian congregations sponsor primary schools. The Armenian community is, however, greatly reduced from what it was in the early years of the twentieth century, when there were more than two million faithful in 2,900 congregations with 1,970 parish schools and 460 monasteries across Anatolia. The Syriac Orthodox Church is very small; today there are seven parishes in Istanbul but only one church building. The other Syriac Orthodox congregations use space owned by Catholic churches. Most of the Syriac Orthodox believers in Istanbul moved from the provinces within the last twenty-five to thirty years.

Each of the Catholic judicatories has at least one church in Istanbul. The Latin Catholics belong to churches operated by French, Italian, Spanish, and Austrian missionary orders; two of their church buildings are very large — the Cathedral Church of the Holy Spirit (Salesians) and the Church of St. Anthony of Padua (Franciscans). There are a number of schools, hospitals, and other service facilities run by various Catholic orders. The Armenian Catholics also have a hospital and a high school belonging to a monastic community, which serves the whole Armenian populace.

Evangelical Protestantism has had remarkable growth in the past twenty years, with major support and influence from several missionary agencies unrelated to any of the MECC churches or their partners. There are eight or nine congregations in Istanbul and others throughout the country. These congregations consist of both converts from Islam and Turkish Christians from other Christian communities.

Historical Background

The area now called Turkey has played an enormous role in the development of Christianity. The first seven church councils, all of which were in present-day Turkey, defined early Christian theology. The seven churches of the Book of Revelation were located there as well. Well-known cities such as Ararat, Haran, Antioch, and Ephesus are within the Asia Minor landmass. Most of the Eastern and Oriental Orthodox communities (except for the African branches) have their origins within this area. During the Byzantine Empire, the cathedral church of Constantinople, the Hagia Sophia (p. 208), was the center of religious life for the Eastern Christian world. Then the Fourth Crusade overthrew Byzantium in 1204, and 250 years later the Turks conquered Constantinople. Since then, the Christian communities have played a minority role, even under the relative benevolence of the early Ottomans. During the last years of the Ottoman Empire, the Armenian community was virtually annihilated, and during the Republic (since 1923) there have been sporadic periods of persecution. Since 2000 Turkey has undertaken a number of reforms; pressures from Islamic parties to move away from a secular to a more religious orientation in society have mostly been rejected.

Contemporary Circumstances

The Turkish Republic is a secular democracy. The constitution promises complete freedom of religion (although members of all religious groups are legally restrained from wearing religious garb in public). In

Hagia Sophia

Hagia Sophia, meaning Holy Wisdom, is the museum that was a mosque that was a church. Built during the Golden Age of the Byzantine Empire in 537, the church replaced one built by Constantinius in 360 and another by Theodosius II in 415. The current building has suffered damage over the years and been restored, but it is essentially the Byzantine structure. Columns and archways, windows and galleries, all make up this example of the imperial nature of the city of Byzantium/Constantinople/Istanbul, Turkey.

The church became a mosque in 1453 by order of Sultan Mehmet, conqueror of the city, and was made a museum by the Turks in 1935. Six disks inside with the names of God and Muhammad and of caliphs and imams, and four towering minarets on the outside attest to the Muslim use of the building. Very little of the early mosaics is still in place, but a fourteenth-century work (picturing Mary, Jesus, and John the Baptist) is partly visible and considered a masterpiece. The dome is 182 feet from the floor and about 104 feet in diameter, and it is the vastness of the space that is most breathtaking. One can only be impressed by the ability and creativity of the ancient architects and builders.

a nation so overwhelmingly Muslim, Christians experience many constraints, both formal and informal. Of the three largest church groups, only the Armenian has remained relatively stable in the past thirty years or so; significant percentages of the Greek and Syriac Orthodox communities have emigrated.

Ironically the same month that Patriarch Bartholomew issued the 2010 encyclical referred to above, it was necessary for the General Secretary Michael Kinnamon, of the U.S. National Council of Churches, to urge Secretary of State Hillary Clinton to use the moral authority of the United States to assure Bartholomew's safety. The Ecumenical Patriarch, Kinnamon told Clinton, is "isolated and often threatened with violence" in his own country. The European Court of Human Rights urged Turkey to recognize the international status of the Patriarch. The court also called on Turkey to uphold the rights of religious minorities, including the nation's Alevi community that wishes to be seen as separate from Islam.

On the other hand, there had been an easing of the regulations governing how persons officially change their religion and how new churches are established or old ones repaired. Bibles and other religious books are published and sold without restriction. In 2009, the Turkish government assured the Roman Catholic Church that it was extending, indefinitely, permission for worship in the historic church in Tarsus, the birthplace of St. Paul.

Because Turkey is located both in Europe and in West Asia, there are numerous points of confusion and contention about identity. This is true in every aspect of Turkish life — political, social, cultural, economic, and religious. While this confusion is not new, attempts to categorize or label any aspect of life in Turkey require an array of qualifying statements.

Interfaith Activities

Because the Christian community in Turkey is small, there is relatively little formal interfaith dialogue apart from that initiated by ecumenical bodies. Informally, however, Christians are engaged in daily contact with Muslims and many close associations have developed. Some individual congregations have taken advantage of the opportunities for structured interreligious efforts.

Annotated Bibliography

Ahlstrand, Kajsa, and Gunnar, Göran, editors. *Non-Muslims in Muslim Majority Societies, with focus on the Middle East and Pakistan.* Eugene, Oregon: Pickwick Publications for the Church of Sweden (Research Series 2), 2009. 166 pages. Eleven essays on status of Christians in predominantly Muslim countries.

Armstrong, Karen. *The Battle for God.* New York: Ballantine Books, 2001. 371 pages. Examines modern fundamentalism among Jews, Christians, and Muslims — its sources and expressions.

Badr, Habib, chief editor. *Christianity — A History in the Middle East.* Beirut, Lebanon: Middle East Council of Churches, 2005. 934 pages. Designed for college and seminary students, and academic researchers, the book was prepared by Middle East Christian scholars. Also available in Arabic.

Betts, Robert Brenton. *Christians in the Arab East.* Athens: Lycabettus Press, 1975. 212 pages. A study of Christians and the politics of the Arab world up to 1975.

Chammas, Joseph, with Archbishop Lutfi Laham, editor. *The Melkite Church.* Jerusalem: Greek Catholic Patriarchate, 1992. 163 pages. Background (prior to 1724) and history of the Melkite Church to 1990, including relationship to the Roman Catholic Church.

Cohen, Raymond. *Saving the Holy Sepulchre: How Rival Christians Came Together to Rescue their Holiest Shrine.* New York: Oxford University Press, 2008. 308 pages, including photos and diagrams. The dramatic story of an international effort to repair the ancient Jerusalem church.

Cragg, Kenneth. *The Arab Christian: A History in the Middle East.* Louisville, Kentucky: Westminster/John Knox, 1991. 336 pages. From early church to present with a look at "A future with Islam."

Dalrymple, William. *From the Holy Mountain.* New York: Henry Holt, 1997. 454 pages. The author follows the journey of two monks who traveled from Egypt to Turkey and then south through the Levant beginning in 587.

Fromkin, David. *A Peace to End All Peace: The Fall of the Ottoman Empire and the Creation of the Modern Middle East.* New York: Avon Books, 1989. 567 pages. A comprehensive history of the modern Middle East from 1914 to 1922.

Horner, Norman A. *A Guide to Christian Churches in the Middle East.* Elkhart, Ind.: Mission Focus Publications, 1989. 128 pages. Descriptions of churches but statistics are outdated.

Irvin, Dale T., and Sunquist, Scott W. *History of the World Christian Movement, Volume I: Earliest Christianity to 1453.* Maryknoll, New York: Orbis Books, 2001.

Jenkins, Philip. *The Lost History of Christianity.* New York: Harper One, 2008. 315 pages. The thousand-year golden age of the church in the Middle East, Africa, and Asia — and how it died.

Keshishian, Aram. *The Christian Witness at the Crossroads in the Middle East.* Limassol, Cyprus: Middle East Council of Churches, 1981. 63 pages. The challenges, promises, and perspectives facing the churches in the Middle East.

Kimball, Charles A. *Angle of Vision.* New York: Friendship Press, 1992. 118 pages. Christians and the Middle East; a broad overview of religion and politics.

MacCullouch, Diarmaid. *Christianity: The First Three Thousand Years.* New York: Viking, 2010. History from 1000 B.C. to the present.

Malaty, Fr. Tadros Y. *Introduction to the Coptic Orthodox Church.* Alexandria, Egypt: St. George's Coptic Orthodox Church, 1993. 302 pages. A definitive history and theology.

May, Melanie A. *Jerusalem Testament — Palestinian Christians Speak, 1988-2008.* Grand Rapids, Michigan: William B. Eerdmans Publishing Company, 2010. 172 pages. The texts of sixty-eight joint public statements issued by the Heads of Churches from Jerusalem on the situation of Palestinian Christians in the Holy Land, into four chronological chapters, each introduced by the author with historical background. The volume also includes an introduction and an afterword.

Prior, Michael, and William Taylor, eds. *Christians in the Holy Land.* Buckhurst Hill, Essex, U.K.: Scorpion Publishing, for World of Islam Festival Trust, 1994. Papers delivered at a conference at Cambridge Lodge dealing with history and with socioeconomic and sociodemographic characteristics of Christians and churches of the Holy Land.

Roberson, Ronald G. *The Eastern Christian Churches: A Brief Survey.* Rome: Edizioni Orientalia Christiana, Pontificio Instituto Orientale, 1995. Fifth revised edition. 252 pages. Descriptions of churches; discusses Catholic-Orthodox relations and contemporary relationships between the Catholic and Oriental Orthodox churches.

Scudder, Lewis R., III. *The Arabian Mission's Story: In Search of Abraham's Other Son.* Grand Rapids: Eerdmans, 1998. 437 pages. Set in the context of Christian mission in the area over six centuries, the book focuses on the Arabian mission as an independent Protestant mission, as part of the Reformed Church in America, and finally completely independent of Western missions.

Sennott, Charles M. *The Body and the Blood.* New York: Public Affairs, 2001. 449 pages. A look at the Christians of the Holy Land and why they are disappearing from the land of Christianity's birth.

Wagner, Donald E. *Dying in the Land of Promise.* London: Melisende, 2001. 277 pages. Palestine and Palestinian Christianity from Pentecost to 2000.

Ware, Timothy (Bishop Kallistos). *The Orthodox Church.* London: Penguin Books, 1993. Revised edition. 359 pages. Summarizes history and faith and worship of Orthodox Church.

Wessels, Antonie. *Arab* and *Christian? Christians in the Middle East.* Kampen, Netherlands: Kok Pharos Publishing House, 1995. Translated from the Dutch by John Medendorp and Henry Jansen. 255 pages. Chapters on major Orthodox and Catholic groups; analysis of Jews and Christians in the Arab/Islamic environment, the mission from the West, and the future of the church.

Wright, J. Robert. *The Holy Sepulchre: The Church of the Resurrection: An Ecumenical Guide.* Jerusalem: Ecumenical Fraternity in Israel, 1995. 27

pages. Bibliography. Diagram of the church with numbers that relate to descriptions of points of interest in the church.

Websites

Arab Group for Muslim-Christian Dialogue; includes documentation on the Abrahamic heritage, religious fundamentalism, and the image of Islam in America: www.agmcd.org.

Armenian Orthodox Catholicosate of Cilicia; includes many ecumenical and interfaith links: www.armenianorthodoxchurch.org/mm/mm.htm.

Christian Information Center in Jerusalem, a Franciscan service to pilgrims of all Christian communities; includes news: www.christusrex.org/www1/ofm/cic/CICmainin.htm.

Churches for Middle East Peace; includes ecumenical and interfaith public statements, and resources, including the "shared Jerusalem" center: www.cmep.org.

Coptic Church, U.S. branch of church headquartered in Cairo; includes link to Pope Shenouda and Coptic history: www.copticchurch.net.

Ecumenical Patriarchate of Constantinople; includes archive of the Ecumenical Patriarch's statements and encyclicals, inter-religious and environmental activities (Patriarch Bartholomew is known popularly as "the Green Patriarch"): www.patriarchate.org.

Forum for Development, Culture and Dialogue, including programs in conflict resolution (including family violence) and civil society capacity building, in several countries including Iraq: www.fdcd.org.

Latin Catholic Patriarchate of Jerusalem; with ecumenical and interfaith links and archives of an important earlier website: www.lpj.org.

Middle East Council of Churches; includes links to many church bodies in the Middle East: www.mec-churches.org.

U.S. Department of State; reports on various countries include current demographic information: www.state.gov/misc/list/index.htm (select country).

World Council of Churches; includes archival and other material including news releases, the Amman Call, the Kairos Palestine document, and links to many member churches: www.oikoumene.org.

Index

Missionaries, missionary activity, xiii,
6, 10, 15, 22, 23, 28, 29, 39, 52-53, 55,
85, 87, 89, 98, 101, 108, 109, 110, 112,
113, 114, 117, 119, 120, 121, 122, 126,
127, 128, 129, 130, 135, 143, 156, 165,
166, 175, 182, 183, 192, 194, 197, 201,
204, 206, 207; American Board of
Commissioners for Foreign Missions, 110, 114, 117, 122; Assyrian
Church of the East, 24, 42, 85, 86,
134-37, 165, 169, 179, 200; Catholic
missions, 15, 39-42, 79, 83-85, 87-89,
98, 165, 192, 206; Evangelical (Protestant) missions, 15, 23, 39-42, 101-4,
106-12, 113-15, 117-19, 121-23, 124-29,
165-66, 192, 196-97, 207; missions to
seamen, 191
Monasteries, monastic life, xiv, 19, 33,
37, 59, 62, 64, 67, 75, 76, 79, 80, 95,
96, 98, 99, 150, 151, 152, 157, 161, 201,
205, 206; first monastery, 157; St.
Catherine's Monastery, 150; St.
George's Monastery, 204
Mongol invasions, 79, 165, 170
Moniur, Rev. Mohsen, 109
Moorish influence, 187
Morocco, 126, 185, 186, 187, 188. *See also*
Maghreb (North Africa)
Moscow (Third Rome), 51, 57, 155, 178,
186. *See also* Russian Orthodox
Church
Moses, 150, 174
Mount Nebo, Jordan, 174
Mubarak, Pres. Hosni, 151
Muhammad, 176
Murad, George, 116
Muslim Brotherhood, 151-52
Muslims. *See* Islam

Nag Hammadi, 153
Napoleon, 39, 150
Nasser, Col. Gabdel Abdul, 151
Nassif, Souad Hajj, 30
National Evangelical Church in Kuwait, 113-14, 130, 190

National Evangelical Church of Beirut. *See* National Evangelical Union
of Lebanon
National Evangelical Synod of Syria
and Lebanon, 49, 114-17, 118, 130,
179, 199
National Evangelical Union of Lebanon, 41, 115, 117-19, 130, 179
National identity, 6, 8, 14, 16-18, 21, 69
Native Evangelical Church (Lebanon).
See National Evangelical Union of
Lebanon
Nazareth, 76, 93, 104, 127, 128, 155, 157,
162; Church of the Annunciation,
155
Near East Christian Council. *See* Near
East Council of Churches
Near East Council of Churches, 23, 41,
102, 130
Near East School of Theology, 116,
119, 123, 180, 182; description of, 182
Nestorians, 63, 70, 110, 134
Netherlands, 80, 212
Netherland Reformed Church, 156
New Sudan Council of Churches, 196
Nicea, 37, 39, 50, 56, 142, 146, 173, 192
Nicene Creed, 25, 38, 50, 52, 57, 92, 122
Non-Chalcedonian churches. *See* Oriental Orthodox family of churches
North Africa. *See* Maghreb (North Africa)
Norwegian missions to seamen, 191

Oman, 189-91, 193, 194. *See also* Persian
Gulf
Omar, Caliph, 33, 39, 61, 158
Organization of Islamic Culture and
Communication, 166
Oriental Orthodox family of
churches, 23, 41, 49, 50, 51, 53, 55, 57,
59, 69-81, 82, 84, 130, 145, 148, 156,
164, 168, 174, 178, 186, 189, 196, 199,
204, 207, 212; common declaration
of, 80-81; description of, 51-52, 69-
70; Oriental Orthodox unity, 70,